Neal-

Enjoy Cowboy Now!

Thanks for the support-

Rhett

COWBOY NOW

Life and Death in the Dim Light of a Patagonian Snow Cave

By BRETT E. CARLSON

Everyman Publishing

Published by
Everyman Publishing
Menlo Park, California
October 2003

ISBN 0-9727910-1-9
Library of Congress Catalog Card Number: TXu-1-006-104

Printed in the United States of America
www.cowboynow.net

To my parents, Doug and Carol, who gave me life.

To Bill Wilson and Dr. Bob, who insure that I stay alive.

"…all stories, if continued far enough, end in death, and he is no true storyteller who would keep that from you."

–Sir Ernest Hemingway

“Patagonia is a terrifying land. For centuries, explorers have been mesmerized and manipulated by her beauty and mystery. For generations she has murdered and maimed the most well-intentioned adventurers. Trapped between two worlds, an Arctic freeze and Pacific winds force hideous weather to erupt into angry storms that blanket darkness. Patagonia’s foundation, the epic Andes Mountains, crawl deep into the southern tip of South America, argued over by Chile and Argentina. Vast oceans and tremendous mountains birth winds more massive than any hurricane, exposing isolation and death. Yet, in their last breath, men are shocked when she kills. I dream of returning soon. That’s her power.”

–S. L. Lasson, National Geographic Explorer

February 27, 1996

The man approached the farmer. He had just leaped from his motorized canoe, which was anchored to a tree two hundred yards along the lakeshore to the west. He was well dressed: jeans, dark blue long-sleeve shirt, working boots, a bright red baseball cap, and pilot glasses. He stood six feet, two inches tall and sported a well-groomed mustache. The farmer noticed and instantly liked the man's oversized, shiny silver belt buckle. The man reached out his hand. The farmer shook it politely.

"Hello," the man said.

"Hello," the farmer responded.

"I understand you have a farm here in this valley, and you run cattle up the valley toward Patagonia during the summer months."

"Yes."

The man pulled a wad of money from his pocket. "I need a favor." The farmer glanced at the money. "I have a group of men coming off the ice field in the next week, and I'll need you to give 'em a lift by canoe to the eastern side of the lake." The man, hand outreached, offered the farmer the wad of money.

"They have been on the ice field?" the farmer asked.

"Yes, for about six weeks now—should come through here in no more than five or six days."

"My friend, go back to the north from where you came. My family has lived here for six generations, working this land and raising cattle. I am sorry, but the storm that just came through here was the worst in the last one hundred and fifty years. Your friends are dead. Go back to the north and forget them."

"Oh no, I assure you they are alive."

"Friend, no person on this earth could have survived the winds and snow that just crossed that ice field—no man, no matter how strong." He paused, and looked east up the valley toward the Patagonian Ice Field. "Up there, people die all the time in much lesser storms."

"I assure you, they lived," stated the man.

"How can you be so sure?"

"While flying a search-and-rescue mission over the region, I saw them!" The man's hand was still outreached, still offering the money.

"Oh my friend, I am sorry, but you saw dead bodies."

This story is the truth. No matter what you may have read or heard about this saga, it is very much a concrete event. These tales and tragedies were pulled from the various journal entries of the nine men who ventured into Patagonia in January 1996.

I am related, by blood, understanding, and family, all of which humbly allow me to give an accurate depiction of the journey. Even in death, stories live forever.

Present Day

My name is Erik *Today* Carlson. My friends call me *Today*. And everything I ever needed to know about successfully living life, I learned from my experiences in snow caves on the Northern Patagonian Ice Field.

I was a twenty-one-year-old college student nearing the end of my education when I decided to take a brief college break. An average American, I had been raised in Los Gatos—a small Northern Californian town between Silicon Valley and the Pacific Ocean. I could have been raised in Boston, Massachusetts, or Bozeman, Montana, or New Orleans, Louisiana, or Miami, Florida. I was an American.

I had decided to join a group of eight other men, ranging in age from seventeen to thirty-five. The goal of our trip was the third crossing of the Northern Patagonian Ice Field, the fourth largest ice field in the world (the three larger ice fields are Antarctica, Greenland, and the Southern Patagonian Ice Field). As planned, the journey in its entirety would take seven weeks. This included packing and preparing, traveling to the region of Patagonia, the actual trek for five weeks, plus debriefing once the expedition was complete.

Of the nine men involved, seven of us were more or less average people. We enjoyed the outdoors quite a lot, but led normal, routine lives. The two men who'd organized the expedition, our leaders, had amassed years of climbing experience. Either of these men could have been world-famous climbers, but neither sought this as his goal. Our story began on January 12, 1996.

January 12, 1996

The flight landed in Santiago, Chile, at eight o'clock in the morning. I had just spent a school semester living in Florence, Italy. I had traveled home to California, packed my mountain gear, and jumped back onto a plane within a twenty-four-hour period. I was tired. I slept most of the flight.

The flight touched down, and I collected my bags and gear. I lugged my gear with me to a restaurant and had some eggs and toast for breakfast, the only thing I recognized on the menu. At eleven o'clock, I boarded my next flight to travel further south, to Puerto Montt, Chile. I was groggy from the long journey and my previous days of traveling.

The Puerto Montt airport was small, so collecting my gear was a simple matter of looking through a heap of baggage that was piled outside of the main terminal. Once through the small, one-building airport, I hired a taxi to drive me the hour it took to reach the city center. My taxi driver drove like he was suicidal. I gripped the back seat like I was on a roller coaster. I attempted to remain calm, but with the taxi frantically dodging numerous buses, swerving to miss roadside cattle, and avoiding a large military truck, I nervously laughed to myself that I could be going to the Patagonian mountains to seek adventure, and wind up killed en route in a taxi accident.

◆◆◆

Puerto Montt was a sleepy seaside village. The main industry was fishing. The taxi drove past the fishing harbor and down Main Street, which was adjacent to the ocean. The driver dropped me at the Hotel Del Mar. Directly across the street was the ocean. The sea was calm. There was no sand or beach, only a seawall.

I walked through the front door. A slender man stood at the reception desk. He was six feet, two inches tall and weighed one hundred fifty pounds. He had hair to the middle of his back pulled into a ponytail. His T-shirt read: *I climb mountains because they're in the way*. I laughed—I hadn't seen that before. Not sure why, but I knew at once that he was part of the climbing team. I approached the front desk directly to his right.

He turned to me. "Hello," he said. "You ready to eat, sleep, and live ice field?"

I was semishocked, and then realized I was a gringo in South America, lugging a large bag of mountain gear. I stood out like a frostbitten toe. "Hello," I answered. "I'm Erik, but you can call me *Today*."

"I'm Michael *Everyday* Bradburn; to my friends, I'm *Everyday*." He was warm and pleasant, and had a peace about him that was uncommon in the modern, fast-paced world in which I was born. His face was covered by a huge smile. "I'm excited; how about you?"

He asked the question like I'd known him twenty years, and in fact, I felt like I had known him for all my life.

"I've been looking forward to this for a year," I answered.

He smiled. "Yeah, that would be about right." He handed the women behind the desk his Visa card. "I'm going to check in, change into some mellow pants, then hit the road, probably stroll down the street toward the port. Take in the sunset. You want to cruise along?"

"That sounds good," I said.

"I'll see you down the road in about fifteen minutes." In one fluid motion, *Everyday* turned to leave while grabbing his gear. His movement was efficient, light, and precise. His body was lean, but his arms lifted his bags with ease and swung them from side to side as if they were feathers. He was strapped with gear as he bolted up the stairs like a gazelle. I watched with amazement.

Shit, I thought. *I have to hike with that!*

I checked in at the reception desk. When finished, I did not leap like a gazelle up the stairs, like *Everyday*, but instead powered my way to the second floor: same result, different movement. Some people are powerful, some are graceful, and others are both powerful and graceful. I moved with power. At my room, I placed my gear in the far corner and grabbed a warm sweatshirt. I was off to watch the sunset.

I walked south down the street. The late afternoon was superb. The sun had started to sink into the ocean. There was a cool, calm breeze drifting in from the Pacific. After about five minutes of walking, I reached *Everyday*, who was casually and peacefully sitting above the ocean. His feet dangled toward the water; it was high tide. I took a seat next to him. He smiled happily at me, then returned his focus back to the ocean. The day had been long, but good.

Everyday was silent as he gazed into the grand Pacific Ocean. Minutes passed. I was unsure why, but it seemed from the start that anything and everything could happen with *Everyday*. The possibilities were endless. I instantly took a strong liking to him.

He lived in Colorado, where he was a rock-climbing instructor during the summer and on ski patrol during the winter. *Everyday* had climbed numerous and various routes throughout Colorado's many fourteen thousand–foot peaks.

He was by no means a professional climber, but he was far, far superior to your average REI customer. This was his first trip outside of America. *Everyday* was a solid climber, a solid human. I knew that I'd be willing to go to war with *Everyday*.

Everyday turned to me. "So have you heard the myth of Patagonia?"

"And what myth is that?" I responded, not breaking my focus from the ocean.

"The crazy myth of the sunshine and weather in Patagonia."

"Not a clue," I said. "I just know that the weather is tragic, alcoholic kind of weather."

"The tale begins thousands of years back, when the ancient tribe Ona, who at the time hung out in the land now known as Patagonia, were out on a hunting expedition. The season had been harsh, so the mood of the tribe was frantic. As the hunt continued, the hunting party approached an open patch of ice resting on a vast plateau, and there, they came upon a poker game—"

"No, not one of these stories!" I interjected.

"Come on, hear me out! Obviously it wasn't a poker game as we know it. The story's been modernized."

"Okay." I smiled. Why object to anything? The afternoon was magnificent.

"So as the hunters curiously approached the game, they noticed that the two gamblers at the table were God and Satan. Instantly, they grew nervous! But one of the angels who was tending bar noticed their apprehension, and motioned for the hunters to enter the gambling realm. So they did. Satan looked bad; he hadn't shaved in days, his hair was red and matted to his head, and a cigarette dangled from his lips. Oddly, even God looked drained. He had shaved his white beard and was sporting a full goatee—"

I chuckled. *Everyday* gave me a sarcastic look, acting like this was the most serious story told since the conception of the Holy Bible. Then he continued.

"Growing a bit more comfortable, the hunters moved close. One of the angels, probably Judas since he looked greedier than the rest, slithered to the side of the Chieftain Hunter. The angel said, 'This particular card hand has been in progress for millennia; they just keep raising the stakes, over and over.' 'What's the bet?' asked the Chieftain Hunter. 'They're betting on the fate and future of these mountains, ' the angel said. 'Both God and Satan are extremely fond of this area. God created Patagonia as the most beautiful mountains on the face of the earth. In contrast, someday Satan wants to turn Patagonia into a strip mall.' Then the angel vanished.

"The hunters stayed to watch the poker game; in fact, they stayed so long they eventually grew old and died. In time, the poker game ended in a draw. After some arguing, God and Satan agreed the mountains would stay and the beauty would last forever, but as part of the wager, the sun in Patagonia was banished for all eternity. The weather was to be horrid and rancid, with the breath of Satan continuously blowing and tormenting travelers."

Everyday stopped his tale and looked toward me. His eyes gleamed like flames. "Patagonia's weather is from the devil. Had you heard that before?"

"The story's new, but I know the weather's piss-poor!" I answered.

"So, as rumor has it, the mountains of Patagonia are the only place on earth that's heaven and hell at the same time."

January 13, 1996

My alarm clock screamed. It was six o'clock in the morning, and I leaped from my cheap, half-stained hotel mattress with searing anticipation. My muscles pulsed with energy. As I walked to the bathroom, I caught a glimpse of my six foot tall body in the mirror. I was tight with muscle, stripped of all excess body fat. I had been training for months, and my legs sensed that all the physical rigors of training—the hill running, weightlifting, biking, and hiking were about to pay off. It was time to begin my adventure, and my body knew it.

I put on jeans, my favorite baseball cap, and a sweatshirt. I got to the café early. I didn't want to sit, so I drank some of the darkest, meanest coffee ever to pass my lips, and then walked to the front door of the hotel. I went through the door like a racehorse out of the gate. I nearly broke into a sprint.

God I'm excited!

The morning street was quiet. I needed to walk off some of my anticipation, clear my face of its excitement. I didn't want to enter the morning meeting with the other men seeming too giddy, too happy, like a virgin boy on prom night. I crisscrossed the city streets, once, twice, and then a third time, just for luck. The city was boiling with the bustle of dawn. The markets were full of life, with shop owners preparing for the day, and hundreds of people weaving their way toward a wholesome day's work.

I smiled. It was eight o'clock, time to meet the team.

I casually, coolly, entered the café—my heart racing.

The group was gathered at two tables, some finishing breakfast, others looking over maps. *Everyday* already had an early audience, and from my interaction with him the previous day, I understood why. Scott *Persistence* Thompson, Tim *Worry* Madson, Pedro *Action* Rodríguez, and Tyler *Slack* Cole all sat casually around *Everyday* in dark wooden chairs.

At a table nearby, looking over a map of Patagonia, was Andy *Direction* Wilson. *Direction* was the man in charge, responsible for the general organization of this expedition. He was six feet tall with short, sandy brown hair and a warm, welcoming face. *Direction's* body was packed with lean muscle. His clothing was modest, but his muscle was not. At thirty-five, he was the oldest among us, and by far the most experienced. He had climbed Mount McKinley, the highest peak in North America, and Mount Aconcagua, the highest mountain in South America, as well as the more difficult climbs in Canada, Europe, and Asia. He looked at me and smiled.

I had found *Direction*.

Next to *Direction* was Sam *Positive* Lincoln, the point man. *Positive* was a legend in outdoor schools across America. He was a hired gun. For any and all extreme training, ranging from ice climbing, rock climbing, mountain climbing, rescue climbing, rope climbing, or tree climbing, basically, if something could be climbed, and people needed to be trained and wanted the best, they hired *Positive*. He climbed fast, strong, and safe. He was five feet, eight inches tall with jet black hair. *Positive's* eyes were deep and dark; his face was cut like fine granite, mysterious like midnight. He was a handsome, grueling sort of man. If I were a woman, I would've fallen in love.

Direction was pointing at a detailed map of Patagonia, tracing a path with his index finger over the colorful paper. "This route will be tough!" he said.

Positive smiled, his deep mysterious eyes peering out from behind a short veil of dark hair. "Yep! But we'll have fun, plus get some exercise while were at it. Should be a good time!"

"God you're upbeat and optimistic!" *Direction* grinned from ear to ear, his face was full of confidence. "I love it!" He had deep trust in *Positive* and sincere admiration.

"Hey, they don't call me *Positive* because the glass's half-empty." They exchanged a short laugh.

I watched intently. *Positive* and *Direction* would lead me into the weather-beaten hell of Patagonia, and I would follow, stride for stride, unto death do us part—that was my role. I was a worker ant.

Against the wall, near the table by *Direction* and *Positive*, leaned Mason *Change* Smith. *Change* stood, arms crossed, staring at absolutely nothing. *Change* was a Canadian Special Forces Mountain Army Ranger. He was physically perfect, a Greek Adonis dressed in mortals' clothing. His hair, aerodynamic in fashion, was a perfectly manicured crewcut. His eyes were covered with dull silver pilot glasses. When the average, paper-pushing family man dreamt of strength, precision, and the perfect balance between height, weight, and muscle mass, *Change* was his vision. He stood six foot, three inches in height, and weighed two hundred and eight pounds. His muscles crept through his tight T-shirt. It was hard not to notice, and right away I knew

Change was a dick. In fact, I could already see that nobody liked *Change.*

I walked toward the main table. The group looked up. Game on!

The first out of his seat to shake my hand was *Persistence.* "You must be *Today*!"

Persistence had a firm handshake. He was a solid man. "I'm *Persistence*; we spoke on the phone last month."

Ah yes, *Persistence.* We had indeed talked over the phone. I had liked him instantly. We had spent an hour one night comparing stories. *Persistence* had strong experience. He'd spent time climbing in North America, Asia, and Africa. This was his first time in South America. At heart, he was a backpacker, but his interest in climbing mountains began directly after a great college-wrestling career. He was five foot, six inches tall, with a bold man's face. *Persistence* was not a huge human, nor was he imposing, but he had solid muscle from head to toe. He looked me straight in the eyes when he shook my hand, and right away I knew *Persistence* could help me through tough and challenging experiences. I smiled as his hand still gripped mine. "Scott *Persistence* Thompson. I was told you'd carry my pack and pull my sled on this little vacation!"

The group laughed.

"From what I hear about you, you're the big dog!" *Persistence* winked at me.

At the same time, both *Worry* and *Slack* stood from their chairs, both their hands outstretched, looking to shake mine.

Slack was twenty-eight years old, with shaggy shoulder-length hair. His aspiration was to be twenty-nine years old. He was a pot-smoking ski instructor from Park City, Utah. His father was a well-known, well-respected bishop in the

Mormon Church in Salt Lake City. In one ski season, the other ski instructors on the mountain gave *Slack* the well-deserved nickname of Preacher Puff; he liked his marijuana. He was an avid backpacker and well experienced. *Slack* had a trouble-free, easygoing way about him. I understood why some people might want to spend hours on the couch with *Slack*.

From behind his shaggy hair, *Slack* casually smiled and shook my hand. "Yo," *Slack* said. "Yo!" I politely responded. He sat back down.

Worry was a master's student in geology at the University of Montana in Bozeman, Montana. He was obsessed with geology, particularly with the geology of Patagonia. *Worry* was in charge of a program for undergraduates that brought students into the northern Rockies for a semester of studying geology. He was oblivious to the fact that the students spent the majority of their free time collecting and eating mushrooms. Back at the university campus, *Worry* was also a floor manager at one of the dormitories. I had been warned that he worried like a New York Jewish grandmother. I noticed he had a very distinct beer belly that had seemed to drift upward into his pudgy cheeks. *Hmm*, I thought, *that extra twenty pounds could get in the way of crossing an ice field!*

I grabbed *Worry's* hand. "I look forward to your technical explanation of why Patagonia's going to kick our ass." He grinned back at me.

"Well—" he started to explain.

Christ, I was joking!

Action jumped forward. Saved by *Action* from the boring babble of *Worry*— probably wouldn't be the last time! *Action* was a spark plug of a human. He was Chilean. And at thirty-four years old, he was one of the oldest. At five foot, four inches tall, he was the shortest. He had dark skin, dark hair, and dark eyes. *Action* spoke limited English, but had a welcoming, friendly face. He was a schoolteacher in the north of Chile. I was told that *Action* had a great ability to get a person out of tight situations.

On my plane flight to South America, I had read a news article about *Action's* older brother. Ten years ago, his brother had left the family home one sunny day in January to attempt to cross the Northern Patagonian Ice Field; his dead body was never found. *Action* felt as if he had unfinished family business in Patagonia.

That was the group. *Positive*, *Direction*, *Everyday*, *Change*, *Action*, *Persistence*, *Slack*, *Worry*, and of course, myself—*Today*. It was apparent, joined together with this combination of men, I could engage and hopefully cross the Northern Patagonian Ice Field. We were a complete functioning unit.

◆◆◆

We crossed the airport runway as the engines hissed. The plane was a smaller, specialized craft, built and designed to land in high alpine runways. It was mid afternoon. As a group, we'd take the Air Chile flight further south to the town of Coihaique, Chile.

"Looks like a short, stubby cigar," *Persistence* said in my general direction.

"You think it flies?" I responded, squinting into the sun.

"We'll find out soon enough."

The plane was small, with seats for only thirty people, and being midweek, the plane was only half-full. Our group made up the majority of the passengers.

Once in the air, I spent the first forty-five minutes of the flight gazing out the window. Chile has an interesting geography. In the north of the country there are high deserts, central Chile is dominated by rolling hills and valleys, and in the south, Patagonia is scattered with high peaks, glaciated valleys, and numerous ocean fiords. Our destination, Coihaique, sits in a high valley surrounded by various mountains.

With no warning, the nose of the plane dropped. My heart rate jumped. Suddenly, the plane decreased in speed. I turned to my left; the sudden jitters of the plane had captured the attention of most of my fellow mountaineers. Once again, the plane lunged forward. My seat belt dug into my gut and held my lower back against the seat. The nose of the plane dipped more.

Christ! I'm not even going to have a chance to die in the mountains. The plane's going down!

My blood rushed. I struggled: nowhere to go. I took a long, slow, deep breath into my lungs. I rolled my shoulders, relaxed my feet, and took another deep, deep breath. The plane dropped in altitude.

I spun backward, looking into the eyes of my peers. Tension! Most of them sat erect, backs straight. I examined their faces, and on some I saw a distinct look telling me they feared death. My breath slowed. My body relaxed. The plane dipped again, pointing to the earth. Not all my companions looked panicked; some seemed calm, as if death were not a curse but a curiosity.

The Chilean stewardess began to scramble toward the microphone on the wall. In perfect English, she spoke rapidly: "This is normal. No need to panic." The rest of the bodies relaxed, as she continued. "My apologies. I forgot to make the announcement that this plane lands in a special manner because of the high alpine valley. My apologies. We'll be on the ground in minutes," she finished with a smile.

January 15, 1996

Five miles outside of the town of Coihaique, Chile, was a two-thousand-acre cattle ranch, owned and operated by Juan Martínez, a fifth-generation cattleman. *Direction* had rented his barn for five days: two days for packing gear and food in preparation for the journey, and an additional three days to debrief once the crossing had been completed. We'd sleep in or around the barn, while spending our days organizing.

Coihaique was west of the Andes Mountains and one hour from the coast. January was warm—it was summer in the southern hemisphere. The hillside gently and casually rose from the valley. The grass was beginning to crisp. Our large, weathered barn sat in the middle of a hill, surrounded on all sides by large grass fields.

The wind soothed my face. I stood, momentarily mesmerized by the distant huge cumulus clouds that bubbled together, creating soft and gentle whites. I turned back to the grass hill. My peers moved efficiently through the numerous stacks of food and gear. The entire hill was covered with various piles. We had been packing for two days.

I stood looking down at fifty pounds of hot chocolate mix. I had been bagging the dark powder for a few hours; it was the last item on my long list.

A tall, slender shadow approached me from behind.

"Seems like a lot of cocoa." I looked to my right. *Slack* was standing, examining my pile of hot chocolate bags as he twirled a strand of his nappy hair.

"Hey, I just follow orders," I said. "And one of the things on my list was two hundred quarter-pound bags of chocolate mix. I just work here! Definitely not in charge."

"Seems like a lot of cocoa." He walked off.

Fifty pounds of cocoa! Jesus! What had I got myself into? I turned around and followed *Slack* to where the group stood in a semicircle. We had worked efficiently for two days. Our excitement kept our pace quick and our steps rapid. *Direction* was making one last check of the supplies. We watched, happily looking over our food and gear. The air temperature was perfect, no humidity. My skin was happy. My body was ready. I felt like a machine ready to mass-produce the model-T.

I smiled. The piles of gear and food looked like some weird obstacle course. There were small piles, large piles, and scattered piles. In total, there were over one thousand pounds of gear, food, and supplies on our little hillside. Most outdoor people love their gear. I mean, they really, really love their gear. They've been known to fondle, coddle, hold, covet, pet, clean, and nearly make love to their gear. It's the damnedest thing. And yes, I was guilty.

Persistence sighed happily and draped his arm over my shoulder. It was as if we were in the presence of the Eighth Wonder of the World. Ice axes, sleds, crampons, ice screws, ropes, helmets, placement wands, pots and pans, sleeping bags, radios, carabiners, hoods, baggies, gaiters, and plastic boots. We had organized and bagged nearly one million calories of pasta, oatmeal, butter, cheese, beans, hot chocolate, rice, flour, sugar, and spice.

Then, as if the moment had never existed, *Everyday* broke

the peaceful silence, drilling us firmly back into reality. "How many damn miles do we have to carry this crap?" He snickered, simultaneously winking at all eight of us.

We laughed. Someone gave me a friendly slap on the back and our heads rolled with pleasure, but at that moment, secretly and silently, the monstrosity of our goal settled down. It was time to go to work!

On our butts and backs, we'd carry fourteen hundred pounds of food and gear for five weeks of climbing. Divided by nine men, that meant each man was responsible for one hundred and fifty-five pounds of portable survival. Since it's nearly impossible to carry that amount of weight in a backpack, and the average large backpack can only lug about eighty pounds anyway, we were also packing three sleds.

Direction finished his sweep of the gear. "Got it all. We're ready to put it in the bus."

Each of us grabbed four travel bags and began to pack and load the equipment into the bus.

There were basically three types of expeditions we could have organized. All three varied in cost, difficulty, and danger. The first would have been to hire porters, which was the norm in most Mount Everest–type climbs. On the average, six climbers would hire twelve or more porters to carry the majority of their gear. In relative terms, this is a fairly fast and efficient way to climb a mountain because the porters haul most of the weight of the supplies, and the climbers climb, setting up the ropes and safety devices. Basically, the porters act as human mules and never see the top of the mountain. That's their job. The climbers climb; the porters haul. The climbers pay; the porters get paid.

The second type of expedition would have been to stash food and fuel drops in the direct line of the route. This would be done either ahead of time, or week-by-week using a plane or helicopter as the group moves forward across their route. An example of this would be longer treks through large areas like Antarctica. This practice allows a team fast, rapid movement because the packs and sleds remain relatively light in weight.

The final means of trekking was our plan. We would move with all the gear. As we pushed through the valley, we'd carry our main gear and set up a camp. The following day we would backtrack with empty backpacks to where our camp or excess stash of gear had been the night before. At that point, it would be late morning and we would load the remainder of the gear stash and haul it past our current campsite. After unloading the stash, we'd then backtrack to our tents, eat, and then sleep. The next morning we would break that camp down, load up, and hike farther up the valley, usually past where our gear would be stashed. We'd make another camp, eat, and sleep—and then repeat the process again. The following day we would hike backward down the valley, once again gathering our gear, and then moving further up the valley. We would continuously leapfrog our gear, day after day, until we reached the ice field. This would take ten to fourteen days.

Once on the ice field, we would use the three sleds. Each sled, fully loaded, would weigh over one hundred fifty pounds, which is a mammoth load to pull with an eighty-pound pack upon your back. We would rotate the sleds among various people during the hiking day. We were not bringing nine separate sleds because the sleds were inconvenient to lug through the valley.

The bus was full of our gear. We took one last look around the ranch, all hoping that when we returned, we would be healthy and successful.

"The ranch has been good to us," *Slack* said. "I think I may miss her."

"We'll be back," *Everyday* answered, while adjusting his ponytail.

"Yes we will!" *Direction* said, covered in optimism.

I believe him, I thought.

◆◆◆

The bus hung close to the hillside road, slithering along like a snake as the driver navigated through the rolling hills of central Chile. The sun was bright and warm. All nine of us sat toward the front of the bus, huddled tight, either engaged in conversation, or looking out one of the windows. I was sitting on the left side of the bus next to *Slack*, who was transfixed in an endless gaze out his window. *Change* sat right in front of *Slack*, in the first seat of the bus, with nobody to his right, peering out of his window like a sniper, also shooting quick, semi paranoid looks over the driver's left shoulder. In the two seats behind me were *Persistence* and *Everyday*. I had perched myself on my knees, facing backward, and was listening to their conversation.

On the right side of the bus were *Direction*, *Worry*, *Action*, and *Positive*.

Persistence spoke with excitement. "Maybe I've watched too many Hollywood movies, but it'd be nice to know my breaking point, you know, feel a little bit like Rambo. Find out what it take to make me throw up the white flag and surrender!"

"So that's it—your reason for coming to Patagonia is to find your physical surrender point?" *Everyday* said.

"That's one of them, but honestly, I've always been good at sports like football, track, baseball, and obviously college wrestling, so I wanted to explore a more isolating physical challenge."

"See what *Persistence* can do in the mountains," *Everyday* said. "See if *Persistence* is a survivalist."

"Get me into the mountains and away from all the eyeballs of the fans."

I laughed. "Yeah, I doubt there'll be bleachers or cheerleaders alongside the glacier."

"You giving me shit?"

"Hell no!" I said. "I'd love to bring some of your college cheerleaders with us!"

"Smart man!"

"So how about you, *Today*, why the long trip away from the warmth of California to the cold ice of Patagonia?" *Everyday* asked.

"I like pain!" I said.

As I answered the question, *Worry* looked at me cross-eyed from the other side of the bus. "You California guys are strange." His round face was perplexed.

"No, I'm serious; pain's like meditation." I sat up just slightly higher in my seat. "When I jog, or bike, or hike, and I push my physical limits, my mind isn't thinking of anything but the pain! No stressing about life, just the pain in my body!"

"Great, really great," *Slack* interjected, looking a bit like Jesus Christ as sunlight christened his head. "I'm going to be trekking with a sadomasochist."

"Not sure I'm that bad," I concluded. "How about you?" I asked *Everyday*. "Why Patagonia?"

He grinned, big and wide, stretched his back, sitting high in the seat, and spoke with confidence and flair. "I like to risk my life unnecessarily!"

"Great, really, really freaking great!" *Slack* said, covered in concern, as he spun backward in his seat. "A sadomasochist and a kamikaze! My experiences in Patagonia should be terrifying!"

Everyday and I looked at each other and laughed.

"So how about it, *Slack*, why'd you come this far?" *Persistence* asked.

"I wanted to experience the isolation of Patagonia, feel the power of the universe," *Slack* answered, his speech slightly slower than the normal man's.

"Oh no!" *Change* verbally attacked, but did not shift his intense glare from the road. "Are you fucking serious! You touchy-feely people are all the goddamn same!"

I laughed, by accident. *Slack* and *Persistence* were shocked. *Everyday* just rolled his eyes.

As if we were under attack, *Change* spun back toward us. I nearly saluted. "The real, and only reason to cross that big piece of bad-ass South American ice: a personal test of strength!" He puffed his chest out another inch as he again wagged his cock! "It's about being a man, being strong!"

Oh Lord! There he goes again, trying to make us fear Change. The rest of us are relating to one another, and he's in the front howling at the moon!

Positive and *Action* had been engaged in a conversation in Spanish directly to my right. I could see some slight concern on *Positive's* face. He understood that the power of *Change* was good for the team, but he also could see that *Change* was disliked.

Positive leaned across *Action* as he spoke. "I've lived down here on and off for years, and no amount of training can prepare a person for the unknown of the weather and isolation. Keeping optimistic in the most horrid situations, always seeing the good, no matter how far down the escalator we descend—that's it for me! Continuing to explore and test my optimism."

"Basically to find out if you can decorate the living room of hell in pretty pastels," *Everyday* said, smirking.

"Something like that."

Action seemed a bit confused by the exact content of our conversation. "Ask *Action*," I said to *Positive*.

"¿Por qué te gustan las montañas de Patagonia?" *Positive* asked, complete with a proper Spanish accent.

"¡Mi familia!"

We understood.

"*Worry*, how about you?"

"I'm excited just to see the area," *Worry* answered. "I only hope the weather's good."

Worry is always focused on things in the future that are out of his control!

I looked at *Direction*. He had been listening to our conversation the entire time, but was still interacting with the bus driver. "So how about it?" I spoke slightly louder, insuring I would get his attention. "Why does our fearless leader continue to lead expeditions?"

Direction paused before he spoke. He smiled, as if he always carried a four-leaf clover in his back pocket. "The New York Yankees, Microsoft Corporation, the San Francisco Symphony, all teenage boys Little League teams, and of course, nine men on the fourth largest ice field in the world—they all have the same goal, a common direction: a defined need to work together." *Direction* took a moment to look at the eight of us, then tilted his head slightly forward. He was happy; his smile grew. "Me, I do it because teamwork under duress is the best kind of unity that I've ever experienced."

Positive began laughing. "That, and you're a control freak." The two men had known each other through all kinds of pleasure and pain. They exchanged glances, no words, just years of history in one look.

I rolled my body back down into my seat, facing ahead once again. I comfortably slid my butt forward. The bus continued to crawl through the hillside. My eyes closed.

January 17, 1996

Over the next two days, we traveled in a boat down the southern coast of South America. This stretch of the Chilean coast was stunning. Steep mountain cliffs climbed from the sea's numerous fiords, and white waterfalls painted the green hillsides. We sailed past deep ocean bays, glaciers, small icebergs, large billowing clouds, rolling waves, and periodic dolphin sightings. I sat on the left stern of the boat and took time to enjoy a free ride.

The boat slowed, and the crew began to shuffle around in preparation. The ocean was calm. There were faint clouds, scattered like cotton, speckling the horizon. I squinted into the afternoon sun and pulled my sunglasses from a pocket. I had been lied to—the weather was good, if not glorious. The temperature was pleasant, neither too hot nor too cold. I took a deep, long breath and smiled to myself. Patagonia's western face seemed pleasant, pretty even.

"One hour!" Somebody yelled.

One hour! I walked to my gear. I vaguely recalled thinking about how people always exaggerate poor weather, and it seemed that Patagonia was no different. The captain stood next to my pile of gear. He smiled at me, a curious smile. I smiled back.

"¡Hola!" I said.

"¡Hola!" he responded, giving me a half-cocked smile. "Good day for hike!" He chuckled.

I began to fidget with my gear.

"¡Amigo!" he said. "You better stop playing with pack."

I looked up. He was pointing off into the distance, toward the sun. "What?" I said.

He pointed at the streaking sun, as if it was the Virgin Mary. "Will be the last you see of her."

I was still bent over my gear, looking off the stern of the boat, my head tilted sideways. The sun was bright yellow, nearly clear yellow. I slowly stood erect. I looked at the captain, and he casually put his hand to my shoulder. With his other arm, he pointed, as if there were a UFO off somewhere in the distance. He spoke slowly: "¡Sun no más!"

◆◆◆

The little dinghy nearly sank with the weight of *Worry* and *Slack*. The two sat side by side, with four extra gear bags in the middle, plus their huge, bursting backpacks resting between their knees. I leaned forward, lowering my eighty-pound backpack into the small dinghy. It sank another inch. I stepped from the boat into the dinghy. *Direction* handed me two additional gear bags. I placed the bags on my seat and sat down on them.

The dinghy pushed away from the boat and forward toward the shore with the weight of the boat driver, Pablo, *Worry*, *Slack*, all the gear, and me. Water skipped into the boat. Pablo efficiently steered the boat toward the beach. As we grew close, we could see that the surf was breaking one hundred yards offshore. Pablo was forced to stop, and we prepared to wade the last one hundred yards.

I swiveled my legs over the boat's edge and into the frigid ocean water. I pushed away from the boat, landing with a slight splash. "Oh that's cold!" I said, guessing the water temperature was forty or fifty degrees.

The water was just above my waist. For a moment, I struggled to get the eighty-pound backpack from the boat and onto my shoulders. Once I had the pack over the rim of the dinghy, it was easier to maneuver and place on my back. I cinched my pack into place, but kept the waist strap loose because I was in the water. *Worry* handed me two extra gear bags. Everything was already wet, and I hadn't even reached the shore of Patagonia. I was not concerned about the contents of my bags because all the gear on the inside was in dry bags.

I turned and headed toward the shore, with my two extra gear bags in tow, each one floating by my side. I plodded along, steadily heading toward the dry beach. After a three-minute ocean walk, I waded through the surf and onto the dry sand. My clothes clung tight to the muscle of my body. I unloaded my wet backpack and sat upon it.

The sun was behind a soft, fluffy cloud, and rays of light shone from all sides. I watched as each of my peers climbed from the dry boat and into the cold, wet Pacific Ocean, walking through the shore break and onto the beach. The day was peaceful, and I was content. Wet and excited, each man walked from the ocean and sat on the beach, waiting as the others sloshed through the water.

◆◆◆

We had all set up many camps before, but as a unit, our work together initially seemed to labor a few steps slow. We'd bump into one another, repeat the same process twice, and nearly tie our hands into knots while constructing our tents.

The nine of us spread our tents over a one hundred–yard radius to minimize environmental impact, as well as give each group some privacy from the other tents. In addition, each group had its own kitchen area. Our domed tents were built for all four seasons, and could hold four people. As I finished with my last task, I paused and looked at the valley.

The mountains rose from the valley floor at a rapid pace. They were covered with a soft shade of green vegetation. The mountain faces lining the valley were too steep to hike, but not vertical enough to climb with rope, that is, by means of technical rock climbing. On the valley floor, there were some slight rolling hills, lots of rocky fields, and scattered marshland. The Tanka River dropped from the higher mountains, snow, and glaciers, through the upper canyons and down to the valley floor. The river was bone cold, just above freezing, and scattered with small to medium chunks of floating ice from the glacier higher up the valley. The silt from the glacier made the river a bright turquoise color, like a deep colorful vein tracing the valley's floor. It was beautiful!

I looked at the other men. They were completing their various tasks. The valley was calm and peaceful, but the isolation of the southern coast of Chile was overwhelming. I watched the others, but at the same time, I felt alone.

January 19, 1996

The hiking day had gone smoothly, and the afternoon was growing old. I was enjoying the fast pace, which gave my legs their first exercise and strain in over a week. My shirt was wet with perspiration. Beads of sweat blotched together on my forehead. *Direction* moved to my right. His stride matched mine. We moved fast, avoiding unstable rocks and veering through short, stubby bushes.

We carried two types of shoes: Teva sandals as camp shoes and plastic mountaineering boots. For hiking in the valley and once we reached the ice, we would wear the mountaineering boots—basically, they're an uncomfortable combination of a stiff, plastic hiking boot and a ski boot. They were heavy, sturdy, and thick because on the ice we would attach ice crampons to the soles.

For a time, I was lost in the rhythm and stride of my legs. *Direction* broke the silence of our rapid pace. "You must get asked this a lot, but how'd you get the name *Today*?"

"You're definitely not the first one to ask, but most people don't," I answered.

"Well, as it would seem, we've got some time to kill." He smiled.

I rubbed my hands together; I hadn't told the story for a

while. "My first couple of years in college, I was sorta crazy with girls, and booze, and drugs—you know, your basic college student."

Direction smiled while avoiding a dead tree stump. His movement was calculated and succinct, no wasted energy.

"But for some reason, I was getting poor grades and not too happy." I looked at *Direction*, as if to say, *Duh!* "I felt like crap. I was always caught up in the dumb crap I'd done the previous weekend. You know, people I'd screwed over, places I'd passed out. And when I wasn't thinking about my crazy past mistakes, I was dreaming of the next weekend and how I'd change the way the last weekend went wrong. Basically, I was trying to live in tomorrow, and sadly obsessed with yesterday. Unfortunately, tomorrow never came, and my yesterdays kept getting worse. By the middle of my sophomore year, I was a wreck. I was lost and in desperate need of a path in life. One night, I met a man named Bill, and this doctor named Bob. They'd been around the block a few times, and could see I'd regularly been shitting all over today, just because I lacked perspective. They taught me how *Today* works."

"What, were these guys psychologists?"

"No! They were just a salesman and a doctor who lived good lives."

Direction seemed moderately puzzled, but allowed me to continue. "After a time, I grew so good at living well in the present moment that everybody started calling me *Today*. Soon, my friends, my professors, my parents, my co-workers, and every single person in my life called me *Today*. I find that if I take everything out of my life—the money, the parties, the jobs, the future this and future that, who and what people think of me—the single thing remaining is *Today*. The here and now! This exact moment in time, and nobody can take it from me. And if I live well today, the future and past instantly take care of themselves."

"Watch that!" *Direction* pointed to some marshland directly in front of our walking line.

"Let's keep our boots dry this afternoon," I said.

"Dry boots are nice," he answered.

January 24, 1996

The valley was behind us. The hiking and ferrying of gear had been long, hard, tedious work. I was happy to be one week closer to the ice field.

As a team, we stood facing the Tanka River. If time were to stop, the river water would freeze, but the rapid rushing current kept the water a dark, turquoise tone. Chunks of ice bobbed and weaved past us. I was nervous. The river was deep and powerful. I looked at the other eight men.

Direction looked at the team. "Okay, who brought the bridge?" He let out a slight chuckle.

"Wait, I think I got the bridge in my pack," *Positive* said, smiling.

Our two leaders were leading, if only by keeping the situation lighthearted.

"That looks really damn cold!" *Worry's* eyes showed fear. "Cold and dangerous!" he added.

"Couldn't be that deep!" *Everyday* said, looking at the group.

"Hey, I needed a bath; this's convenient." *Positive* turned, smiling as he high-fived *Direction*.

"I'd rather smell," *Slack* said, looking back down the valley toward the ocean.

"It's only water, you faggots." *Change* verbally attacked everything when he spoke.

"Hey, my pack is gay and takes exception to your homophobic remark!" *Everyday* joked, his face seemingly carefree. "You army guys sure are bigots!"

"Why don't you and your fag pack kiss my ass!" *Change* turned, broke formation, and began to walk upstream, looking from side to side as if he was in battle.

I made eye contact with *Persistence*, as if to say, *It's going to be a long trip with that idiot around. Persistence* winked at me; we both knew that we secretly hoped *Change* would wander upstream and get lost for a while!

Direction bent over and grabbed a large rock, about the size of a big cantaloupe.

"Here's to good luck." *Direction* kissed the rock, and then hurled it high into the sky. Tumbling, turning, rolling, it peaked and headed downward like a dart into the middle of the river.

Kerplunk! No other sound, just the rock splashing angrily into the water. *Direction's* shoulders drooped slightly, and his eyes darted left and right, scanning the river's shoreline. His mental gears were in overdrive. Right where we stood the water was too deep to cross. We knew because if it were shallow, the free-falling rock would've clanked upon the river's bottom. We'd heard nothing except the initial splash.

"Great, really damn great—we found the deep end!" *Worry* frowned; his hair, clothing, and attitude were all disheveled. In the last few days, as the weather became worse and comfort became a phantom, his every word dripped with disappointment.

Rapidly and efficiently, the team spread out along fifty yards of river shoreline. From the river's shore, cannonball sized rocks flew into the sky, then back into the river. I walked another twenty yards up the riverbank. I was about to grab another rock the size of a bowling ball when *Direction* and *Worry* walked up from behind me. They were talking.

"This thing looks deep!" *Worry* was saying. "Too cold and too deep to cross!" *Worry* nervously shook his finger, darting it frantically in the air.

I made eye contact with *Direction*. He winked at me, and I stopped. *Direction* spoke calmly with a concern I had yet to hear in his voice. "People who've been in this valley before say there's no easy place to cross."

Worry spoke fast. "Shouldn't we try to look north, scout maybe, or hike a day and look?" His eyes rapidly and fearfully examined the river. His tone grew increasingly fearful. "I mean look at that!" He sporadically gestured at the river.

Oh Christ, he can't be serious!

Direction was patient and tolerant. At that moment, he was a far better leader than I could've been. He calmly relaxed his arms, palms to his side, peacefully exposing his chest. "*Worry*, you hold that thought." *Direction* turned toward me. "*Today*, I owe you a story. Earlier this week, you told me how you got your name *Today*, and now I'm going to tell you about a cowboy called *Now*, and his new calf named *Life*—"

I rested back on my heels. I watched *Worry's* face as *Direction* talked to me. *Worry* focused on *Direction's* lips, hanging on his every word.

Direction began his story. "As it's told, every morning the Cowboy *Now* would eat a good breakfast and drink some strong cowboy coffee. Cowboy *Now* was a young buck, practicing to be a world-class calf roper. Cowboy *Now's* mother was called *Nature*, so after Mother *Nature* would fix the Cowboy *Now* his breakfast, he'd leave the house and go to the corral to practice his calf roping. Cowboy *Now* could rope any calf. He had practiced and practiced, and was a great calf roper. But this particular day a new calf was delivered to the ranch. The calf's name was *Life*. Cowboy *Now* attempted to rope *Life* all day, failing every time. After a long and unsuccessful afternoon, Mother *Nature* stopped by the back corral. 'How are you, my son?' she asked. Frustrated, Cowboy *Now* answered, 'That calf's got too much damn energy. I can't rope *Life*!' Mother *Nature* looked at her frustrated son and spoke sweetly: 'Cowboy *Now*, haven't you been paying attention? This is your test. This calf called *Life*—once you rope her, you will be ready. Don't expect *Life* to sit still and let herself be roped. *Life*'s going to run, and fight, and pull, and kick, and seemingly avoid your rope. Your job, Cowboy *Now*, is to anticipate when and where *Life* is going to turn, adjust to where *Life* will run. Sometimes you will anticipate when and where *Life* will change direction. Other times, you'll be taken off-guard and you'll just have to adjust your rope while *Life* is turning back to the left, or bolting to the right. But if you focus, Cowboy *Now*, you will rope *Life*.' Mother *Nature* continued. 'My son,' she said, '*Life* will never be out of reach; she's in a fence, available to all who earnestly seek her. *Life* can always be roped—that I guarantee." And with that, Mother *Nature* finished with a smile!"

Worry looked at me, baffled. "That was beautiful!" he said. "Look at me, I'm all emotional and junk, but I don't understand—"

Direction interrupted. "Tell you what. When we find a place to cross, *Today* will cross the river first; you can watch, make sure it's safe!"

"Not sure I want to watch *Today* die either." *Worry's* face showed signs of hope. The vexing wrinkles in his forehead were gone.

"*Today*, you going die this afternoon?" *Direction* asked, smiling at me from only one corner of his mouth.

"Nope!" I answered, simple and concise.

"Good, then it's settled," *Direction* finished.

I nearly broke into campfire songs with a strong verse of "Kumbaya My Lord," but instead I heard the call from up the river's shore. "I got it!" someone shouted. I spun back around to my left, and focused to the north.

Positive stood forty feet away from me with an enormous grin on his face, a grin which must have equaled my smile the first time I ever saw a girl's breasts. "It's shallow enough here." He waved his arms in the air. "We can cross here."

That man is always upbeat!

I walked over. "What are you so happy about?" I asked *Positive*.

"An ice cold river crossing!" His head bobbed up and down, looking a little psychotic. "Icy cold! Nothing better!"

The others arrived and, in unison, we grabbed rocks. Simultaneously, rocks flew high toward the clouds and, after cresting, rapidly accelerated back toward the water. *Kerplunk, kerplunk, kerplunk, kerplunk*—it was like Pearl Harbor. A chorus of clanking directly followed the onslaught of rocks.

We'd found the spot where the river was most shallow, but it was still moving far too fast and powerfully for us to enter and cross one person at a time. Safety in numbers would be our theme, and we planned to cross in groups of three.

Direction pointed to me. "*Today*, you and two others scout the river crossing!"

I'd known what was coming, and I understood that I needed to be solid in mind for the benefit of *Worry* and possibly others on the team who might be feeling doubtful.

I wanted *Everyday* and *Positive* to scout the river's bottom with me. I felt most comfortable with those two, and jumping into a rapid, freezing river wasn't my idea of relaxing. But as a team, we were still creating unity, and I knew I had to spread my trust.

"*Slack*, *Persistence*, time to get wet!" I motioned for the two of them to join me along the shore. I grabbed a nearby stick, six feet long and two inches thick. I would lead the way across the river, constantly assessing the direction and depth of the river with a stick and my foot.

Linked tight at the elbows, *Slack* on my direct left, with *Persistence* connected on his far left, we slid into the frozen water. The water rushed past my legs and into my boots. "Holy crap!" I hollered. The others laughed aloud from the shore, as they sat dry, organizing the gear. I yelled back at them. "Yeah, yeah! Keep laughing—you're next, you bastards!"

The water hit *Slack*. "Wow dude!" He choked on his words.

I moved a little farther, up to my knees. My foot was pushed side to side. The current increased.

The water filled *Persistence's* boots. "This's crazy!" he whimpered.

I looked over, *Positive* stood on the shore, smiling at the three of us. "Yeah, nothing like a river crossing to wake ya up in the morning." He smiled sarcastically, but I had to admit he was right. I was alive, no doubt about it. The water rushed past my thighs. My breath began to labor. My lungs struggled to find air. I gasped, reaching and poking with my stick. My feet fumbled, feeling and touching, scouring the river's unseen bottom. Walking by Braille. Inch by inch, I slipped into deeper water. The deeper I got, the more I was forced to use my stick as well as *Slack's* arm. I jabbed fiercely with the stick, while pulling tighter and tighter against *Slack's* arm. The water hit my groin; my face curdled with pain.

"Snowballs!" *Positive* howled with laughter.

Kiss my ass! was all I thought.

Ten minutes had passed. Ten long, grueling, freezing cold minutes, and we were only halfway across the River Tanka. My feet were numb, and my legs were growing weak from the freeze. In my mind, the motorcycle of fear had been kick-started, and it was racing circles around my brain. Panic was near. The powerful water was just below my chest. This was madness.

Total insanity!

I leaned forward hard and tough into the strong, deep current. The other five men had finished organizing the gear and stood watching from the shore. They had grown silent. Their jeering comments had given way to concerned looks. My feet barely clung to the river bottom. The water contorted my direction. My breath struggled to find rhythm.

Suddenly, surprisingly, uncontrollably, my body jolted forward as my foot slipped, losing its fragile grip on the river bottom. Instantly my chest hit the water. My jacket was ripped open, and freezing water rushed against my skin.

"Fuck!" I screamed, water filling my mouth. My legs rushed downstream, flapping violently in the nagging current. I pulled tight on *Slack's* arm. He pulled back. My nose jerked forward into the water. My mind chanted death. The freezing water tugged and ripped. My right shoulder went under, my left shoulder went under, but still my hand clung tight to the stick. My forehead began to sink. Panic bubbled from my mouth.

Without panic, death would come easy.

I yanked upon *Slack's* arm. I cranked my head toward the sky while water flushed through my clothing. *Not dying now!* I pulled my chin from the icy water and, at the same time, realigned my feet, pulling my right foot under my body while aggressively jamming my stick into the river's bottom. Back on both feet, I forced myself to breathe deep.

Persistence yelled at me. "Hey!" I looked at *Persistence*. His face was wet, but his face was confident. "We're fine, halfway there. Keep moving!" he said with blue lips.

I believed him. He was in the water with me; he understood. His face was confident and strong even though he was cold. I paused. For a brief moment, I took a deep breath, and then another breath, followed by one final breath. I mentally focused on the months of preparation I'd done to be ready for such moments. *Persistence* was right; we were moving in the right direction, frozen and numb, but in the right direction. I moved my foot another six inches. I controlled my breathing.

Some rivers in life are tough to cross, some rivers are not—and some rivers end up being only streams. Rivers come in all different sizes, shapes, strengths, depths, colors, and levels of difficulty. Some can be crossed alone, and some can't. There are rivers scattered throughout the world, and despite their uniqueness, they're all similar. One thing that's true about every river on planet Earth: Eventually, they all have a dry shore on the opposite side.

I walked onto the dry rocks, with *Slack* and *Persistence* directly to my left. We were out of the water. I was frozen—the coldest I had ever been in my life. The others stood on the opposite shore, applauding our crossing. It took the three of us twenty minutes of total concentration and dedication, but we had succeeded. We had just crossed the River Tanka.

I ripped open my pack, pulling fresh clothes from the dry sack. Stripping, I was naked in moments. My skin was a bluish, pinkish tone. I hurried to cover my bare skin. Shirt, sweater, bottoms, socks, hat, jacket. The dry clothes were great, but after being that cold, for that long, clothes were nowhere near enough to turn around the dangerous process of hypothermia that we'd set in motion during the river crossing. Time to generate heat. The three of us broke into a slight jog, moving up the riverbank. The best way to cure cold arms, cold legs, and a cold body was to create blood flow. We jogged north up the riverbank four hundred feet, and then back down. We repeated jogging until some warmth returned.

Once I was warm, I began to set up camp. I started to boil water as *Slack* and *Persistence* set up the tents. As I worked, it dawned on me how easy it would've been once we crawled from the water to sit down on the riverbank and get colder and die. We were halfway there, rapidly moving into the second stages of hypothermia. To avoid disaster, we took simple action. Movement created warmth.

On the opposite river shore, the other six men entered the water. One by one, *Positive*, *Direction*, *Change*, *Action*, *Worry*, and *Everyday* each squealed in pain.

I stood, dry and happy, yelling and heckling them loud and proud. "Nothing like a cold bath in the morning to clean behind the ears!"

Previously, *Slack*, *Persistence*, and I had crossed with light, efficient packs, bringing only the bare essentials of tents, dry clothes, and hot drink equipment. The other five men were crossing with packs loaded full of gear. And this turned out to be better because it weighed them down, forcing their feet to the river bottom. All six had watched us cross fifteen minutes earlier. They knew the crossing was very attainable; they'd just watched three people succeed. Knowing we'd succeeded and accomplished the feat gave them a great mental edge.

The six others crossed in fifteen minutes and emerged from the water with blue, chattering lips. The tents were ready and the hot water was boiling. They changed into dry clothes, ran up and down the riverbank, and then, as a team, we drank hot chocolate.

Ice and snow began to fall from the clouds. We all retreated into our tents and sleeping bags. It was two o'clock in the afternoon. There was still food and gear on the other side of the river. We'd warm ourselves, rest for an hour, and hope the weather would blow past, allowing us to ferry the rest of the gear across the river in sunshine.

In Patagonia the terrible weather never seemed to pass, and in fact, on that day, it only grew worse, much worse. After an hour of warming our tired bodies, we dressed back into our cold, wet, soggy clothes, put our saturated boots back on our feet, and exited the tents. I stood for a moment in the strong, dismal rain. The hour of warming my body vanished in a moment. I was once again shivering. As my foot hit the icy cold Chilean river water for the second time that day, I couldn't help but think and laugh at all the people who have a romantic, exotic, delusional idea about mountaineering. *Bullshit, mountaineering is cold and miserable!*

January 25, 1996

Glacier Nosla was eleven miles across at its widest point. The glacier snaked its way through miles of rocky cliffs and frozen, cloud-covered peaks. As it climbed through the valleys, it splintered into various directions. Some fingers of the glacier led to the Northern Patagonian Ice Field, and other fingers led to the base of various mountains such as San Valentín, Mt. Leinad, Mt. Nivek, and Mt. Kaj. We would hike the Patagonian finger. Our route kept us on Glacier Nosla for twenty-five miles of cutting and carving through the various séracs, crevasses, and icefalls.

While eating our morning breakfast, the nine of us gathered in a semicircle, ready for a geology lesson on glaciers. We had agreed to let *Worry* give an hourlong talk.

"Glaciers are alive—they're moving, ever-changing creatures." *Worry* was excited. "They're also hungry and deadly!" *Worry* spoke of glaciers like Nosla as if they were needy, drunken women.

"Hey, just as long as this one's not alive while I'm on it!" *Everyday* joked, while thumbing at his beard. Unfortunately, he couldn't have been further from the truth.

Worry continued, his proud face shinning with academic

knowledge. "Glaciers are huge chunks of ice that move slowly over land. They form in cold polar regions and in high mountains. Glaciers range in thickness from about three hundred feet thick to nearly ten thousand feet thick." *Worry* paused and looked around at the group, and we were still paying relatively close attention. "There are two main kind of glaciers: continental glaciers and valley glaciers. They differ in size, shape, and location. Continental glaciers are wide, extremely thick ice sheets that cover vast areas of land near the earth's polar regions. This type of glacier can bury mountains and plateaus and conceal the entire landscape except for the highest peaks. The Northern Patagonian Ice Field is one of these glaciers, and it has built up at the center of this region and slopes outward toward the sea in all directions. The other type of glaciers are valley glaciers: long, narrow chunks of ice that rest in high mountain valleys. Many of these are either moving up or down a valley."

I began to daydream. Traveling and hiking on the lower glaciated valleys of Patagonia presented different types of problems than did traveling on the ice field. In the lower valleys, the glaciers were covered with many, many crevasses, some small in width, maybe one foot across, and others larger, twenty to thirty feet in width. But all the crevasses in the lower valleys had one common trait: They were below the firn-line, or current snow level, which made them exposed and open, not covered by snow. This allowed us to see them clearly and identify the danger. And since we could see the hazards, there was no need to rope together in teams of three. We hiked, most of the time at our own pace, as we avoided the danger of the icy graves. Usually, the team would split into separate groups, depending on our various paces.

During the first few hours of our hike that day, the nine of us managed to split into three separate groups. *Positive*, *Everyday*, *Change*, and I began a fierce and competitive pace toward our campsite. A half-mile behind us were *Direction*, *Persistence*, and *Worry*; they pushed steadily forward, feeling no need to accelerate up the glacier at a race pace. And a mile back, *Action* and *Slack* had slowed to take some photos. For Patagonia, it was a nice afternoon, with high clouds, no rain, strong wind, and miles of visibility. But still, the sun was nowhere in sight.

Our little group hiked in a line formation. The pace was rapid and aggressive. Even in the dominance of nature and mountains, men's egos can surface. *Change* moved past *Positive* and increased the pace to a rapid, repetitive march. *Positive* followed, directly behind his heels. *Everyday* and I kept in stride.

The glacier was carved with crevasses. Our feet shuffled and danced around and over the small ice gashes. We walked the length of the larger crevasses, cutting across where it was narrower. We had forward motion marked by slight zigzagging. Our feet jumped, glided, and avoided trouble as our heads focused ahead. Another hour passed; all four of us showed no signs of slowing.

Two days earlier, when the team was lower on Glacier Nosla, *Positive* and I had hiked a hill to the north of our campsite to get a better view of our position. After a painful hour of hiking directly next to *Positive*, just prior to the hill's crest, he accelerated at a pace that was inhuman—a pace I could not hold. I was humbled and more than impressed, because before that I had always been the man to push the limits.

Now *Positive* clipped along nearly in the shadow of *Change*. *Positive* was built low to the ground with solid legs, and when he moved, he moved with power and authority. *Change* also moved with power. *Change* was all about power. He admired the strength and body of *Positive.*

Everyday was thin. His legs were like a gazelle's. He moved with grace, purpose, and precision. His step never labored; it was always in unison with his breath and the rest of his body.

After an hour and a half, the pace again crept up a notch. Faster and faster our feet shuffled, dodging and avoiding danger. Looking at *Everyday*, I could see he'd grown tired of *Change's* macho demeanor, his fuck-you attitude, and his general character. *Everyday* dropped his head, pushing the pace. I followed, as *Change* dropped slightly behind *Everyday's* left shoulder, and I kept in stride off his right shoulder. *Positive* followed behind the three of us. Secretly, he knew he was the king of the mountain. Once more, *Everyday* found a faster, more efficient pace, churning his legs, pulling the weight of eighty pounds on his back with what seemed like ease. My lungs pulled in the thinning mountain air. The lactic acid seeped into my strong thigh muscles, causing an intense pain because my circulatory system was not delivering enough oxygen to my leg muscles. A solid pain began to fill my body. I glanced at *Change*; his face labored, his mouth gasped wide, sucking and needing air.

Pain's the best humbler.

With over eighty pounds strapped tightly to his back, climbing a slight hill, *Everyday's* step moved one step closer to a jog. My head dropped, sweat dripping from my weather-burned nose. *Everyday* unzipped the side zippers on his pants, exposing his lean leg muscle to the open mountain air. I lifted my shirt, exposing my lean stomach muscle.

This is not fun! There was no reason for this insanity.

I trudged forward. The next five minutes crawled past; time felt like an eternity. Nearly three people wide, we pushed the pace, *Everyday* still at the point, *Change* and I his wings. The ice was becoming uneven, unstable. Numerous little crevasses lingered on both sides of our trail. Sweat dripped into my eyes; my step became blurred. *Someone should stop before one of us gets hurt.* I looked to my left. *Change* had closed his eyes—too much pain. I thought for a moment: *What the hell is he thinking?* I thought about speaking up, but no, maybe, no. Should I ask? Pain can confuse. Too late!

Change's left foot clipped the edge of a crevasse. He stumbled, tilted to the left, and fell sideways toward the ground like a dead tree. *Change's* left hip slammed into the ice and ricocheted slightly, as his butt slipped and filled the opening in the ice. The crevasse was only two feet wide. His backpack tilted against the far side of the crevasse wall. His stomach faced the sky.

Everyday, *Positive*, and I stopped. Gasping, I struggled to control my breath as blood gushed through my heart and body.

"Goddamn it!" *Change* screamed, his eyes raged red with blood. "Goddamn you!" Both the veins in his temples pulsed.

I leaned forward, hands on my knees. My legs throbbed. I was exhausted.

"You assholes!" *Change* continued to scream.

I looked at *Everyday* and *Positive. Curious reaction.* Using my forearm, I wiped snot from my nose.

Positive offered his hand to *Change*. "You want help?"

"Fuck no!" *Change* yelled, pointing at *Everyday*. "And fuck you!"

"Are you joking!" *Everyday* said, looking down upon *Change*. "You dickhead! You started this adolescent cock-measuring contest!"

Change was tired, but continued his rant "Look at you! I don't get this crap!" His breath labored as his head dropped back on his pack.

"What?" *Everyday* asked.

"I don't get it! Your legs are like goddamn toothpicks!" *Change* replied. "You look like a goddamn telephone pole!"

Everyday managed a slight chuckle; *Positive* smiled.

"So that's what this's about. Your army crewcut against my hippie ponytail?"

"Goddamn right!"

"You're a fool!" *Everyday* smiled, attempting to make light of the situation.

Change paused, attempted to move, and became convinced he was stuck, butt into the ice. He was defeated, but still ranting. "My legs are twice, maybe three times the size of yours," *Change* pleaded. "I'm trained, full of muscle and you listen to goddamn reggae music!"

Everyday had caught his breath and checked his ego. "It ain't about the muscle, you musclehead." *Everyday* was relaxed as he spoke. "It's not muscles that climb mountains. It's this!" *Everyday* tapped upon his head, his long hair dangled. "It's mental, you moron!" Both his eyebrows were raised.

"That's bullshit! I'm an Army Ranger!"

The wind was calm. The gray clouds had crept lower in the valley. Patagonia was altering moods. *Change's* breath had slowed.

"You're right," *Everyday* answered. "You're one strong Army Ranger, and when you hike, you think of yourself as the strongest Army Ranger. I understand. You're superhuman. But me, I think of myself as a mountain goat!" *Everyday* looked to the north at a nearby snowcapped peak.

"Man! I think of myself as king of the mountain goats." *Everyday* offered his hand to *Change*. "And my friend, your Army Ranger butt is stuck in the ice, and the hippie mountain goat's up here, offering a hand."

Change reached forward, locking hands with *Everyday*. They made eye contact. *Change* stood and began to adjust his disheveled pack.

"Goddamn hippie," *Change* said with a smile.

"Goddamn Army Ranger," *Everyday* answered while brushing the loose snow from *Change's* back as he joked. "*Change*, my friend, muscle's good for one thing, going out to the bar to get yourself laid for a night, but for walking, I prefer my brain." *Everyday* laughed, as he pointed to himself. "I'm funny."

◆◆◆

My sleeping bag was comfortable. My body was tired. The last ten days had chipped away at my body's strength. I was exhausted, but I was still having problems closing my eyes and getting to sleep. The day had been warm, but in the last two hours, as one more Patagonian night descended on us, the temperature had dropped forty degrees.

Suddenly, the silence was broken by a loud, frightening *POP,* followed by a deep rumble.

"What the hell's that?" *Persistence* asked.

"Avalanche," replied *Change*, his voice groggy.

"What!" *Persistence* shot up in his bag, frantic.

"Calm down, and let me sleep." *Change* was tired. "We're in the middle of an eleven-mile wide glacier; no avalanche could even come close to us."

Before any of us could argue with him, there was another *POP*, then two more consecutive *POPs*, followed by a fourth *POP*. The ice beneath our tent hummed with energy, while it shook and pulsed slightly. A constant rumble filled the Patagonian night sky.

"Man, that's spooky!" *Persistence* said.

"When the temperature goes from warm to cold, the way it did tonight, that causes all the snow to release. That's the popping we hear—the release of the snow. The rumble's the actual tumbling of the snow." *Change* was half-asleep. "Now let me sleep; the hippie tired me out today."

Silently, I laughed and closed my eyes. Poor *Change*!

Five minutes passed. My mind slowed; sleep was near. There was something calming and chilling, simultaneously, about listening to the mountains of Patagonia release avalanche after avalanche. The power was immense and all-encompassing. I slept well.

February 1, 1996

We crested a slight hill. The gray clouds hung low, pulling toward the earth and ice. I removed my glasses and stopped walking.

"Oh yeah!" someone yelled from the front. We had arrived. We were at the northwestern end of the Northern Patagonian Ice Field.

The sky was thick and full of pressure. The ice was flat. Compacted tight, between the ice and sky, a sliver of horizon extended from side to side as far as the eye could see. You could feel the pressure created by the clouds pushing down upon the hard, frozen ice pack. Ninety percent of what my view was of ice and clouds. I placed my glasses back on my face—no change. White and gray.

We gathered as a group, removing our packs. The Northern Patagonian Ice Field had been crossed two times. The isolation of the region, the domineering winds, and the massive prolonged blizzards all combined to cause adventurers and mountaineers many failures in their climbing endeavors. Patagonia did not want to be tamed.

It was our turn to attempt the third crossing of the Northern Patagonian Ice Field.

February 7, 1996

I woke up. It was day twenty-one. We were three weeks into the journey. The morning weather was miserable. The rain tapped repeatedly and consistently on the tent. The wind shuffled our tent flaps.

For the last week of travel on the ice field, we had been shrouded in a thick, heavy coat of white and gray. I desperately missed the sunshine. We hadn't seen a landmark, or mountain, or anything to judge our position since we hit the ice field a week prior. We had been walking, attempting to judge our speed and compass direction by where we presumed we were on the map we carried. For a week, we had been living ten to fifty feet at a time. That was our range of sight. The rest of Patagonia, the rest of the world, was a phantom. We had talked about it, dreamt of it, told stories about it, but slowly and surely, we were forgetting the existence of all colors but white and gray.

Outside the tent, as if on cue, *Positive* began to sing "Amazing Grace." Unfortunately for me, he sang very loud, strong, and happy. "Amazing grace, how sweet the sound!" *Positive* was fifteen feet away from my head, cooking oatmeal in his snow kitchen. I wanted to kick his ass.

Slack's ratty head and fully bearded face peered out of his sleeping bag. "Is that guy ever, just once, not happy about life?"

"Nope! He'd find something positive during a nuclear holocaust," I replied.

I was awake, but I was definitely in a poor frame of mind. My body was worn out. I was grimy because my pale skin hadn't seen the sun or a shower in three weeks. My morning mood steadily decreasing, I made a mistake and created a mental list of my wants: a cup of rich, flavorful coffee, a stereo playing good music, a pillow for my head and not a smelly coat rolled into a ball, a pair of shoes instead of plastic mountaineering boots, and last, a car to drive. I was tired of walking.

Fifteen feet away in their snow kitchen, *Persistence* joined *Positive*.

Positive's happiness flowed freely. "I got everything I need, right here and right now!" he said, in a colorful, upbeat tone.

"And what's that?" *Persistence* asked.

"Some warm food, a direction to travel, and good traveling companions."

Suddenly, it was as if he was heckling me, as if he'd heard my mental list of wants.

"That's all you want?" *Persistence* asked.

"Those are my needs, not my wants, and besides, it could be worse. I could be lost with no shelter, no food, and no friends."

The wind pushed the tent to the left; it didn't move, but almost. The rain poked and prodded.

Positive, since I'd come to know him, hadn't even *hummed* a negative tune! His body, his face, his persona remained always and continuously happy and upbeat. He was contagious. Prior to this, in my normal, everyday life away from Patagonia, I'd considered myself an optimist. I was now being forced to reevaluate my criteria.

Slack ripped and pulled at his North Face sleeping bag; finally his hairy head disappeared back into the bag's belly. Discouraged, I rolled back to my left. *Ah, how nice, the warm spot in my sleeping bag.*

Outside in the rain, the wind rolled and pushed our tent. The weather had found a steady, miserable rhythm. Gradually, the snow camp came to life. One person at a time, people dragged themselves from their tents and joined the others in the wind, rain, and ice.

I had grown frustrated with thinking, so I manipulated myself into a moderate state of motivation and changed into some warmer clothing. I was up and moving despite myself. As I walked into our snow kitchen, I rubbed my eyes. The morning was wretched, thick with clouds and moisture. I was groggy, and combined with the poor weather conditions, the world was a blur.

In the rain, I ate hot oatmeal with warm butter and drank hot chocolate. As I finished my oatmeal, my bowl began to fill with rain. I was still cold, and my body felt fifty pounds overweight. It was time to break camp. After three weeks, we were efficient: pack tents, pack kitchen gear, store garbage, organize personal gear, rearrange the sleds, and if needed, prepare the rope teams. Slowly my body came to life. The weather showed no signs of compassion, remaining thick and murky.

In what seemed like moments, the group was organized and ready to move forward. "Ten minutes," someone shouted. Ready to hike, I bounced in place to keep the blood flowing through my body. My hat was pulled low and tight, covering my ears. As I bounced, I watched my breath. *Pant! Pant! Pant!* My breath floated freely like a ballet, momentarily hanging in the open mountain air and then violently, helplessly shredded into the vast cauldron of Patagonia.

The wind tormented us. I stood between *Action* and

Everyday. Bounce! Bounce! Pant! Pant! Waiting to tie into the rope team, I listened to *Everyday* sing to himself.

"I am climbing mountains for Jesus!" he sang, while bouncing as if he was on a pogo stick.

The wind played tricks with the words. "You're not even religious," I retorted, too cold to be entertained.

"Yeah, but I hear Jesus isn't biased," he yodeled at me like a crazy Swiss man.

"You're whacked!"

"My son, Jesus also likes the whacked!" His bounce increased in height and speed. "I'm climbing mountains for Jesus, Oh yeah! Wearing crampons for Christ. Oh yeah!"

I grabbed my backpack and in one swift motion lifted it to my back. Eighty-plus-pounds settled down. I strapped in, ready for pain.

Everyday spun around in a full circle, hands toward the sky, ponytail spinning, "Ladies and gentlemen, the Patagonian Boys Choir asks y'all to join the hymns for the Almighty." He continued, "Climbing mountains for Jesus! Oh yeah! Wearing crampons for Christ. Oh yeah!"

My backpack strapped tight, now laughing aloud, I made some slight adjustments to my pack while listening to *Everyday* ramble about Christ and crampons, choirs and churches. My task for the next couple of hours would be to haul one of the one hundred forty–pound sleds. I yanked the sled into place and attached it to my hips.

Hips, don't fail me now! I had eighty pounds of gear and food pushing down on my backpack waist belt and a one hundred forty–pound sled pulling backward on my hips. Over two hundred pounds, pushing and pulling my hips apart, I was definitely not going to break any speed records.

The four sleds were known as pigs. I'd been told it was an

old mountaineering term, a very, very appropriate mountaineering term. The pig sucked. When I pulled it, I felt like a dog on a leash. I hated pulling the pig.

"How's the pig?" *Worry* asked as he walked past, moving toward his rope team.

"She's not called pig because she's a daydream," I responded, taking notice of his red, weathered cheeks.

As I made my final adjustments, I swung back around, and confronted my pig. "You be a good little piggy this morning"—I pointed at the sled—"why don't you go wee, wee, wee, all the way home and let me ride your pork ass!" I'd be packing a lot of baggage that morning.

The rope team moved. I moved! Here we go! Rhythm and thought!

In life, all people have their own pigs to pull. Some pigs weigh five pounds, and other pigs weigh hundreds and hundreds of pounds—you could think of these as psychotherapy levels. Normally, during the day's movement, there was no scheduled time to pull the pig. It always seemed that magically, at the exact moment moving forward seemed near impossible— the pig was released. One hour passed; I pushed on! As I walked, the ice crunched beneath my plastic boots. My eyes searched and scoured the horizon for something, anything to focus upon. Nothing! Two hours passed. The lactic acid slowly began seeping into my legs, causing more pain. My body's six senses became acute. More ice crunched under my boots. *Crunch! Crunch! Crunch!* My breath began to struggle; my lungs burned. A deep ache attached to every single muscle in my body. Slow and steady, again, and again, and again. *Crunch! Crunch! Crunch!* Slow, steady, again, again, and again. If I thought crying would relieve the pain, I would've shed tears. The repetition was horrendous, like Chinese water torture. *God help me!* My rope stopped. It was over!

At one point in my life, I actually liked the outdoors!

◆◆◆

I was pigless. We moved on. The eighty pounds in my backpack felt nice, light, convenient. I casually strolled, as if I were on a springtime walk, as if I'd just let go of a lifetime of hate. *I hated that damn pig!* For fun, I skipped once and then twice—light as a feather. In my joy, I didn't notice the wind was growing. The visibility had dropped to thirty feet. The lead rope team had vanished into the white abyss. Oddly, I felt like it was a nice day. I no longer had the pig. I worked myself into a steady pace. My eyes canvassed the white horizon, searching for anything besides nothing. Whites and grays, grays and whites, white-grays and gray-whites, the horizon melted together. I could not discern any difference between ice and sky. The day was blending.

Time passed and we stopped for some water, and a rest. It was eerily silent. I casually watched my peers. My body was tired. I looked around at the guys who were pulling their pigs, only to discover that I admired watching others pull their pigs. It gave me a better understanding of the strength that was required to pull a pig from point A to point B.

Visibility had dropped to twenty feet, just far enough to see the other two men on my rope team. The wind was fast at sixty miles an hour, strong enough to put me back on my butt if I didn't focus. I pulled my hood tight to my head. My rope moved, and I began to walk.

The Patagonian Ice Field was flat. So as we started to climb a slight slope, I silently began to worry. The pace had slowed to a crawl. I understood. The people who were hooked into the pigs couldn't climb a steep grade at any sort of rapid pace.

Slowly, all forward movement stopped and visibility dropped to zero. No movement! No sight! I kept looking at my rope, waiting for it to move and force me forward. I kept waiting for my queue to hike. Zero! I was blind. I was alone. *Shit!* I couldn't do anything but wait. The wind grew stronger. Five minutes passed, ten minutes passed, and now my muscles were cold. Patagonia was coming together, there was a storm brewing, heaven and hell were about to fight, and I stood alone. My brain began to chatter at me. Without my permission, fear crept in.

Direction walked at me, out of the white clouds. "We're lost," he said with no emotion, squinting his eyes to keep the wind and ice out.

Damn it! We're lost.

"There's a huge crevasse at the hill's crest that could eat a house!"

"Why we on a hill?" I yelled because the wind was roaring and I needed to be heard.

Direction paused for a split second, just long enough for me to see fragments of fleeting indecision in his eyes. "Good point!" he said, continuing his descent past me.

Moments later, *Worry* walked past where I stood planted, swaying in the wind like a weed. "We're lost!" he repeated, his jacket's hood singed tight around his head.

I looked toward the ice; my boots had a fresh layer of snow building up on their plastic exterior. Out of the white stumbled *Change*, nearly falling, scrambling to stay in control of the pig behind him—downhill, pigs were known to sprint. He was the last man on that rope team. "Pig!" he yelled, jostling with it, but losing, "No pig!" He attempted to pause briefly to look me in the eyes. He failed! "Fucking pig!" The pig was running. The pig was winning, defeating and deflating *Change*. He vanished, and again I was alone.

The wind pushed me to the left. I stepped back, just in time to be pushed to the left again. *Everyday* moved past me in total silence. As my climbing rope snaked past my feet, I spun back around and descended a few hundred feet, back to where the ice grew flat.

Once on level ground we probed the snow for crevasses or ice bridges. No danger, so we unhooked from our ropes and dropped the packs into the snow. *Action* removed his shovel from the back of his pack. There was a huge crevasse up the hill from our position, and we were lost. A blizzard was settling down, gathering power. It was time to dig into the ice and create shelter from the storm. *Action* began digging, creating one of our shelters from the wind.

Action has always been about creating a solution to the problem.

I followed *Action's* lead, digging a tent pit. As I dug, the wind grew in intensity and fury. I paused, looked around for a moment, and realized that a massive storm was in its early stages. I continued to work, digging the pit an extra foot deep so we'd have more protection from the storm—hopefully ensuring that our night of survival would be uneventful. I knew the winds of Patagonia, in ghastly weather, could burst at over two hundred miles an hour—stronger than a gigantic, world-class hurricane.

February 10, 1996

We had been pinned down by the storm for three nights. My eyes opened to a constant demon like hiss. The sun had not yet risen. I guessed it was five o'clock in the morning. The world was dark, but the incessant rage and fury of a three-day Patagonian blizzard roared on. Outside the tent I could hear a continuous shoveling; nothing had changed. It had been two hours since the last time I'd shoveled snow. I'd managed to sleep for forty-five minutes. Not the best rest, but it was enough time to give my brain forty-five minutes of respite from the storm.

The last three days had progressively grown worse. The first night was actually exciting. Staying awake for an entire night, shoveling in the darkness to save our tents would be a good story once I returned home from Patagonia and sat around a warm, dry dinner table. The second night of sleep deprivation and shoveling added to the legitimacy of the storm story, but frustration and fatigue were developing the tale further than needed.

The third night was coming to an end. All my clothes were wet. My sleeping bag was wet. And after the chaos of the last three days, snow and ice had covered nearly every inch on the inside of our tent. Mental fatigue was surpassing physical exhaustion. Our main goal of protecting our tents had grown into a three-day battle, and as we grew more physically drained, we'd crawl into our wet sleeping bags still dressed in snowy pants and wet jackets. After passing out for an hour, we crawled back into the blizzard for more shoveling. Everything was wet—clothes, sleeping bags, hats, socks, and gloves. We desperately needed a break from the storm and some time to dry our bodies and bags. No relief was in sight!

I crawled from my soggy sleeping bag, exiting the shrinking tent. Three days prior, the snow pit had been four feet deep, built and used as protection from the terminal winds of Patagonia, but after the last three nights of fighting the blizzard, it was ten feet deep and growing. The ice field was miles upon miles of flat ice, so as the snow tumbled across the flat surface, it continued forward until it was stopped or trapped. Our pit of protection had been transformed into the perfect catch basin for all the snow particles floating on top of the ice field. For three days, as the snow fell into our pits, we shoveled it out, creating a volcanic effect. The walls grew, and what once protected us from the uncontrollable elements of the storm was strangling us.

I grabbed the shovel from *Slack*; chunks of ice clung to his thick beard. His lips were severely chapped. No words, just the passing of the metaphorical torch. Immediately I began to work, clearing the snow ramp that lead into our pit. The snow was ruthless, never-ending. I worked hard for thirty minutes. My breath labored, so I paused, realizing my life was about to be forever altered: I watched the snow, inch by inch, creep higher and higher, accumulating faster than any human could shovel. The walls of my tent were collapsing.

I refused to surrender to the weather. I was strong. I shoveled faster, and faster, and faster! With my mind racing, I forgot to breathe. My rapid actions arose from panic, but they masked my pain and fear as determination.

I made two quick passes up and down the snow ramp, shoveling at a frantic pace. Then I moved to the tent where the tent walls were fifty percent collapsed. Round and round the shrinking tent I went, nearly jogging. Once, twice, and then a third time. My breath labored; my lungs burned. My exhausted fingers curled around the shaft of the shovel, frozen and brittle. I looked around. I looked at myself. I was a ruined wreck—exhausted, deflated, sweaty, wet, and lost.

It's pointless! The snow was climbing higher and higher. I needed something positive. I required reassurance. I needed a syringe full of hope injected into my freezing veins.

At the top of my pit, swaying in the blizzard like a strong redwood tree, stood *Positive*, the happiest, most upbeat, most optimistic human on earth.

"Hey!" I screamed to him. Nothing! I moved slightly closer, screaming once more. "Hey!" *Positive* spun backward, looking down into my hole.

Wait? I'm confused, what's on his face? "Hey! How we doing?" I yelled.

"WE'RE FUCKED!!!" *Positive's* face nearly detached as he screamed back.

Boom! Reality! My brain came crashing down upon itself, like a black hole; the weight was too much to allow any movement. Death was my reality, growing and evolving, as I moved toward my last breath.

I retreated in the direction of my dying tent, throwing myself at the tent's door. Snow sloshed into my face. I ripped at the door, throwing my head inside the tent. *Action* and *Slack* were violently shivering, squeezed tight, shoulder-to-shoulder, contorted uncomfortably close by a shrinking tent. *Action's* dark Chilean skin looked pale and soggy. *Slack's* stringy, wet hair hung gnarled over his face. They both stared blankly at me.

"What?" I asked.

"What?" they said.

I jumped back to my feet and ran back up the ramp. Instantly, the wind knocked me into the air, flipping me head over heels. Struggling, I rolled over, crawled to my knees, and began to crawl on the ice. I couldn't see anything. I was frantic, maybe lost. Shuffling along like a dog on my hands and feet, I scampered into *Positive*.

Positive was digging. He looked at me. "GO GET A SHOVEL! TIME TO GO UNDERGROUND! TIME TO DIG A SNOW CAVE!"

I crawled back to the pit. The tent was gone. The blizzard had eaten our tent. *Action* and *Slack* stood silent, mesmerized and amazed that the tent had been destroyed so efficiently.

One more time, I grabbed the shovel, took a final glance at *Action* and *Slack*, and crawled back into the blizzard. I was a white smudge on a white wall. I was on autopilot. I had to be—there was nothing left. Physically, mentally, and emotionally I was bankrupt. I rolled into *Positive's* fledgling cave, synchronizing my shovel stroke with his. I dug for survival. Stroke by stroke, snowflake by snowflake, we dug a huge, protective snow cave.

◆◆◆

The team filled the cave. Not much was said, but we all knew that a poor situation had gone from bad to horrible. Out of the frying pan and into the ice!

Our shelter was strong and well built, and would hold all nine of us. I sat on my butt, wet and cold. My knees were raised with my arms resting on them. In front of me sat *Action*, *Slack*, *Positive*, and *Direction*. The others were struggling through the storm to find the large cave.

At that moment, the five of us in the cave didn't realize it, but up above in the storm, *Worry* was flying through the air. The wind had launched him like a rocket. Dramatically, headfirst, he came crashing through the roof of our snow cave. *Worry* lay crumpled at my feet. He had crawled from the remains of one of the snow pits, stood erect, and been lifted by a massive wind gust and thrown well over twenty feet. Our shelter had been pierced by a careless *Worry*. The cave was weaker, but it appeared it could still be used. We built a miniature igloo around the hole in the ceiling. *Worry* was frozen and dumbfounded.

The group was in horrible condition, both mentally and physically. The storm had taken charge; we were forced to react, to survive, to dig a snow cave and go underground. We sat in a circle, our backs to the snow cave wall. The last three days of battling were a wash. The storm was ruthless. In my life, death had always been tomorrow. It was time to face the man in the dark.

I looked at the eyes of my peers. *Positive* was silent, dead silent. *Direction's* face was blue, and he had removed his boots to attempt to massage warmth into his frozen feet with vigorous strokes. *Change* had pulled his hat over his face; his bluish-white lips chattered. *Everyday's* straight-ahead gaze looked spent. *Worry* looked dumbfounded. *Slack* sat next to him, head drooped in defeat. *Persistence* was to my left. I briefly made eye contact with him and saw that he was not ready to die on that day.

Breaking the silence, *Change* shrilled, "No!" Tears began to role out of his tired eyes, and again he made an obnoxious shriek, like a pig being butchered. "AHHHGGGG!" Nobody had a response, because we understood.

I looked up at the ceiling. A crack had begun to form in the snow roof. The pressure of *Worry* had weakened the structural integrity of the snow cave. In time, the cave would collapse. I was cold to the bone. I was afraid to die. I had years of schooling, I had learned countless lessons about life, and all my knowledge at this point was irrelevant. Intelligence was futile. My lips were blue, my blood was cooling, and the only thing I knew to cure these were movement and action. Movement would warm my body; action would warm my mind.

My decision was based on survival. I didn't want to be a hero.

"That crack stretches the entire shelter; it won't hold!" I said. Defeated, frozen eyes gazed back at me. "Some of us need to go back into the storm and build another cave. Who wants to help me dig?" I asked.

Persistence raised his chin.

Hours earlier, *Positive* had shown me how to dig a shelter when it appeared life was ending. Now it was my turn to pass this impulse on to *Persistence*. We crawled to the cave's entrance.

Patagonia was savage. Hell had been raised. I peered my head out of the cave, looking to my left, and then back to the right. The ice attacked my face. Visibility was zero. The winds blasted at over two hundred miles an hour, stronger than anywhere else on earth.

Dear God!

I stood. Was I stupid? Blasted! A firing squad of chaos threw me into the jet stream of wind, snow, and ice. My body twisted as I was nearly launched into orbit. *Oh tumbling tumbleweed!* Back to earth I hurled, jammed headfirst into the snow. Ice scraped and peeled skin from my forehead and nose. My feet flapped in the open wind.

At least my face is out of that awful wind.

I yanked my head from the snow. Blood dripped from my nose and forehead. *Oh shit, that ice is sharp!* I spun to my right; I spun back to my left. *Could I be two feet from the snow cave entrance? Or a hundred feet? Am I lost?* A drop of deep, red blood rolled from the tip of my nose; it fell onto the white snow. One drop of red in an ocean of white. I was lost.

"*Persistence*!" I screamed. Not a sound was made, the wind robbed my words before they left my mouth. "Hey!!!" It was as if my head was crammed into a pillow. I rolled to my left. Death was all over. I rolled back to my right and perched myself onto my butt.

The ants were upon me, fear crawled and etched its way into my brain. My mind screeched! My heart pounded. I wanted my mother! *God Help Me!*

Time to move. I couldn't just stay, ass planted into the ice, and freeze to death. I rolled to my left and adjusted myself to my knees. Before I left that spot, wherever that spot was, I needed to mark it, to ensure I didn't get even more lost. Having nothing—no extra gear, no wands, not anything to leave as a home base—I unzipped my pants and urinated.

Bright yellow is home.

I crawled forward, like a child. My mind raced, like an adult. In life, when everything is hunky-dory, talk, theories, and philosophical bullshit are easy; the true acid test comes when the anthill has collapsed and the ants have begun to scatter frantically. Can the ants regroup, forget about theories, or philosophy, or the right thing to do when you're in a coffee shop just moving your lips, barking at life from behind a fence? When chaos strikes, how many ants die before a direction is found? Death was near, and my fear had mixed with life's regrets, creating pure panic. Cold sweat oozed from my pores.

I crawled ten feet forward. As I moved, I looked side to side. White! Covered by more white! After ten feet, I circled back one hundred and eighty degrees. I crawled straight back, looking for the patch of yellow snow. It was beautiful to see my own urine. But I was still lost!

I'm screwed, I thought as I crawled straight past my urine, examining it, verifying that it was mine, and that it was not going to be covered with new snow in the next minute. *Yes*, it was my urine, and *yes*, it was still yellow enough.

Ten feet out, ten feet back. White. White. White. White. Once back at my urine, I turned directly to my left. This time, I crawled faster. I was growing numb and at the same time, I worried that I was losing my better judgment. *Or is it normal to use urine as a landmark?*

Out of the all that white, I saw blue. Stooped low, *Persistence* was wearing a blue hat as he peered out from the main cave. His eyes darted, left to right, right to left, and then he smiled. I moved close. *Oh, I love blue.*

"Don't do that again!" he said.

"No, I won't," I answered.

We moved out of the cave. *This time, stay low*, was my only thought. The wind whipped at our backs, slavery. We continued to crawl, linked together, until we reached the top of one of the snow pits. An hour ago, it was fourteen feet deep, but it had been filled with snow and was now four feet deep.

I rolled down the ramp and stood. I thrust the shovel into the pit wall. My plan was to dig straight into the old snow pit wall to build our cave. The first cave was too large, making it susceptible to weakness and problems. This cave would be smaller; it was clear we'd need to make three smaller, more stable caves this time.

I was cold. My movement was labored, slightly slower; the freeze had slowly settled into my skin and bones. My shovel's head pierced the snow, briefly controlling a pile of fresh powder. I threw it over my head. For five minutes I frantically wailed away at the snow and ice. The cave entrance was done. I was warm, or warmer. I looked at *Persistence.*

He'd been by my side, doing jumping jacks to increase his body's warmth. He looked slightly blue. I handed him the shovel and moved to his left. Without hesitation, he thrust himself straight into a deep, hard shovel stroke. I jumped in place to stay warm and shook my arms frantically, up and down and side-to-side.

I stood at the new snow cave entrance, looking into the blizzard. We'd rotated digging the cave in shifts of ten minutes. This allowed us to keep warm, as well as stay out of the other's way while we shoveled inside the cave.

At the top of our pit, *Action* crawled out of the blizzard. He tumbled down the snow ramp toward our new cave. "Here!" he said while handing me a second shovel. "How is cave?" he asked with a cold Spanish accent, his dark eyebrows covered in snow.

"Coming along," I answered. He looked confused. "Good!" I said, keeping my English simple.

"Big cave very weak. Hurry here!" I didn't need to understand his words; his eyes told the story.

Action gave me one last look, laced with concern, then disappeared back up and into the white. I crawled into the cave. "Hey, we need to work faster. I'm coming in to help dig!"

Packed extremely tight into our developing snow cave, contorted oddly on our backs and sides, we chiseled away at the snow. Rhythm took over and time vanished. I was aware of the possibility of death on the surface, in the stronghold of the storm, but I was consumed with the task at hand. My mind dug in the snow and avoided digging mental pitfalls for itself. At that exact moment, I was calm.

Persistence said something, but it was muffled and hard to hear. I cocked my head toward him. "Say again?" I requested.

"What's your proof of life?" *Persistence* said again, his breath labored.

"My what?"

"Your *proof of life*."

"Not sure I understand." I could feel my forehead wrinkle with questions. "What do you mean?" I asked without breaking the rhythm of my shoveling.

He readjusted his shovel grip. "It's the exact opposite of a *cross to bear*. You understand that, right?" He wedged his shovel firmly into the snow. "When a person has a cross to bear in life?"

"Yeah! That I understand."

"So if a person's *cross to bear* is some problem or fiasco they must deal with in life to live and function successfully on earth, the opposite of that is their *proof of life*." *Persistence* paused, stopped shoveling and looked at me.

"And?"

"It's what makes you, you. What makes you happy! Something that reminds you you're alive and well!"

"What's your *proof of life*?" I asked.

"I'm good at helping people through their problems. Comes natural to me."

"*Persistence*—the great guide through troubled waters!"

"So, what's yours?"

"I write good," I said.

"You write well," he corrected me.

"Yeah, that! But I've always enjoyed using English incorrectly. It's liberating!"

◆◆◆

I was underground. My body worked as my mind wandered aimlessly in thought. Simple pleasantries like warm summer days, convertible jeeps, sandy beaches, ice cream on hot summer nights, T-shirts, sandals, miniskirts, and my mother serving cold iced tea.

Unfortunately, I was brought back to reality when *Persistence* accidentally elbowed me in the side of the head. "Oh sorry," he said.

"No problem," I answered. "I was daydreaming of summer, and it's probably better I don't fantasize too long."

"Yeah—" *Persistence* was interrupted by *Positive's* yelling.

"Big cave's down! We're in trouble up here!" *Positive's* voice carried into the cave.

"How's everyone?" *Persistence* yelled toward the cave entrance.

"*Direction's* hurt!" *Positive* answered.

"How bad?" I asked.

"It's his neck and hypothermia; he was buried when the cave collapsed." I swiveled around; *Positive's* head was peering into the cave. "How long 'til you're ready in there?" he asked.

Positive looked panicked. "Five minutes!" I touted. *Positive* disappeared.

Flustered, I turned back to *Persistence.* "Holy Christ, you see that; he looks like hell!" I said.

"You should see your eyes!"

My heart rate was now at one hundred and eight-five beats per minute. It was confirmed: I was afraid to die. I was human. I grabbed the shovel; frantically and rapidly, I continued to sculpt the cave. I was not a Catholic or Protestant, Jew or Mormon, Muslim or Buddhist, but as I felt the sap of fear drain into my body, I began to pray.

God help me? God help us! God help me! God help us? Desperation is boring, patient, and deceitful.

My shovel worked faster. *God help me, God help me, God help me!* Prayer came easy; death was near.

◆◆◆

One of the new caves was finished. It was definitely not perfect, but good enough for survival. *Positive* helped *Direction* into the cave and I put him into a wet sleeping bag, which at that point was the only kind of sleeping bag we had.

"You stay with *Direction*. Warm him up; warm yourself up!" *Positive* said with a glimpse of slight hope in his eyes.

My focus returned to *Direction*, as I rapidly rubbed his arms and shoulders, generating friction and heat.

"Hey!" *Positive* said. I looked back at him. "Don't die!" he said, winking with a mischievous grin.

"Thanks, you bastard!" *Jesus, that's all I need— to die!* *Positive* pushed his way up and out, back into the storm.

Persistence crawled over *Direction*. "I'm going to the top to help the others dig," he said, following *Positive*.

I pulled a stove from one of the gear sacks. Quickly and efficiently, I created fire. Placing a full pan of ice onto the flame, I added some water from one of my bottles to help it melt quickly. I was going to need lots of hot water, and fast. My plan was to put bottles of hot water in the sleeping bag with *Direction* to increase his body temperature. Once the stove had begun to melt the ice, I pulled a bag of hot chocolate mix from the storage sack. In addition to the warm water for his body, I would make *Direction* hot chocolate. In five minutes it would be boiling.

"My grandfather was a minister," *Direction* said.

"I'm not religious," I answered.

"Neither am I. But my granddad crawled around the beaches of Normandy in World War Two, comforting the dying, talking about God while he experienced hell!"

Sometimes it's hard to tell the difference between delusional and spiritual.

He continued. "After the war, he didn't talk much about it."

"I understand!" He seemed coherent.

"At the time, we lived in the Central Valley in California, and every week he'd take his sermon into Folsom State Prison. Bad place, bad men. When I was eighteen years old, one night he pulled me aside, and we went to the back porch. At the time, I didn't know why, but he knew that he was close to death. He sat me in a wicker chair at the far end of the porch, by the large oak tree. For the first time in his life, he told me stories of death from the invasion at Normandy. He talked for hours. I listened! The dying at Normandy, he told me, all had one thing in common. As death grew near, they prayed to God, whether they had faith or not. All the fearful, bloody men that he held in his arms while they crossed through the gates of death, prayed to God. All men, no exceptions!"

Direction took a moment to look me in the eyes. "That same night, he told me about the men at Folsom State Prison. He'd listened to hundreds of men at that prison, and the one constant behind those stone walls he said, was that not one of those men felt like they'd been given a fair shot at life. All those murdering, raping, thieving men felt they needed more luck in life, a better draw. The scum of society wished for luck. The dying heroes at Normandy prayed to God."

He stopped; his eyes floated, soft and gentle. *Was I supposed to understand?* I placed a bottle of warm water under his armpit and began to mix hot chocolate.

After a moment, his gaze recaptured mine. "In life, you'd

better be a prayer or one lucky bastard."

◆◆◆

The nine of us disappeared underground and into three snow caves. We vanished. That was our only choice for survival. It was simple; the path before our feet led underground and into the ice. Above, on the barren, ravaged, open ice, the storm raged. It grew more massive, more punishing, more horrendous. Patagonia had created a tremendous, evil monstrosity of a blizzard. No human or creature could have survived on the surface. The wind blew in gusts well over two hundred miles an hour. The snow blew horizontal for miles. The mountains and rock were beaten. The sun was banished. It was a permanent midnight. And in the middle of the storm-ridden Northern Patagonian Ice Field, nine people lived in three snow caves.

February 13, 1996

The cave was tight, wet, cold, and dim. At night it was pitch black. During the day, limited daylight was able to transfer through the snow ceiling.

A snow cave must stay fairly small in comparison to the number of people inhabiting it. The warmth of human bodies is the best and most efficient way to generate heat in the cave. The snow ceiling must be rounded in a dome like shape. This spreads the weight evenly, creating better structural integrity. The roof should only be one or two feet thick, which is still thick enough to trap the heat, but not too thick to add too much snow weight upon the roof. If possible, the cave entrance should be lower than the main cavern to insure that rising heat remains trapped in the cave.

In our snow cave, our shoulders touched when we lay flat on our backs. When rubbing shoulders grew tiresome, sleeping on our sides was the only other option. Our heads were six inches from one wall, and our feet were nearly rubbing against the other wall. Bits of snow got into everything, like sand at the beach.

Action crawled from his sleeping bag. His dark face was covered by a black beard. From three feet away, I watched him intently. The idea of personal space had been lost. For the last few days, *Action* had performed the same routine every morning. I watched; there was nothing else to do. He crawled to the far end of his bag, turned back around, and straightened his entire bag, as if he were making his bed. Sitting back down on the end of his sleeping bag, he put on his pants, boots, jacket, hat, and gloves, just as he'd done the day before and the day before that.

More and more, it was apparent that *Action's* English was inadequate to the task of expressing his fears of death and the torment of his uncontrolled thoughts. As I watched my Chilean friend, I slowly and surely understood why, *Action* had created a regular morning routine just the way people do in their ordinary daily lives: a morning cup of coffee, a newspaper, a workout, or an afternoon nap. Many people also find comfort in communication, but *Action* couldn't speak effectively, so he built and created routine. Routine provided comfort, even in two hundred mile an hour wind. After he put his clothes on his body, he'd grab one of the shovels and dig, clearing the entrance to our snow cave. *Action* could not speak of his concerns, so he kept his mind calm by shoveling.

I looked to my left. *Positive* and *Slack* were starring straight into the snow ceiling. *Slack* had his finger firmly lodged into his nose, rooting around for a booger or just entertaining himself; either way, I understood. I heard movement and looked back just in time to see *Action's* feet scampering out of the cave.

"That must be tough." I said, wondering if *Positive* or *Slack* would know what I was talking about.

"Tough—that's inspirational!" *Positive* added.

Positive understood. *Action's* routine masked his inability to communicate.

Positive continued gazing into the snow, not breaking his concentration as he spoke. "Imagine not being able to say,

'I'm afraid to die.' We've talked about death all the time over the last couple days." He sat up. "Death! There, I said it! But imagine for him—not being able to say the word, or communicate the gut-wrenching fear. He's a strong man."

"Reminds me of my uncle," *Slack* said, breaking a two-day spell of silence.

"What?" I asked, remembering *Slack* could speak.

"*Action's* daily routine makes me think of my uncle Dean and the time I spent with him in the hospital, just before the cancer slowly ate him to death."

I was taken back. "My condolences." What else could be said?

"He was in the hospital on and off for months. During that period, I sat and talked with him. He was a great storyteller. One of his stories that really stuck in my mind was the tale of Gus."

Since this was the first time *Slack* had shown life in days, he had my attention! "So tell us!"

"Gus was gathering firewood one day, away from his village, and he came across a demon. Instantly, the demon sensed Gus's displeasure with life, and realized he had a live one on the line. So the demon made Gus an offer. He'd live the rest of his life in constant pleasure—basically endless sex, drugs, and rock-and-roll—but at the end of his life his soul would belong to the demon. Gus leaped at the chance and proceeded to live the rest of his days engrossed in endless and sinful pleasure. He was in heaven, so to speak." *Slack* smiled at his own wit.

"Then the day of Gus's death arrived. Once Gus was in hell, the devil placed him at the base of a hill; he planned to make Gus push a large round boulder up the hill for all eternity. So Gus's damnation began. After much strain and pain, Gus would reach the summit of the hill, but once at the top, he'd magically find himself at the bottom again, forced to repeat the process, over and over and over and over.

"One day, Satan was surveying his operation and came across Gus. At that point, Gus had been damned for thousands of years. So Satan, being the Supreme Smart-ass, asked Gus how he was enjoying his damnation. Gus paused, casually and coolly rested his arm against his boulder, and responded happily: "Yeah, be safe to say I enjoy my boulder rolling. It's good, wholesome work; everyday I know what I'll be doing, and it gives me constant purpose and routine." This infuriated Satan. And he immediately banished Gus from hell, as well as outlawing all routine. Hell's never been the same since!"

I was shocked. "Good story!" I said, as I looked toward *Positive*. *Slack* was elegant. He was concise. He spoke with authority.

"So in this hellish storm, routine's comfort," *Positive* said.

Slack nodded yes.

"So what happened to Gus?" *Positive* asked.

"He was banished to earth, and now he's known as *Addiction*. He spends his eternity forcing people to repeatedly climb hills that they dread, over and over. Really, he became a thief, because when he settles down upon a person, he robs them of their ability to choose."

"Bastard!" *Positive* injected, as he leaned forward and the muscle under his tight undershirt flexed.

About that time, belly-first like a penguin, *Action* came sliding down the snow entrance. He rolled over, sat up on his butt, and shook his head, clearing the snow.

"Simple routine. Amazing!" *Positive* said. "I've always held my emotions inside me when I probably should've communicated. After this hell, I'll speak about what bothers me."

"Let's teach *Action* some English."

◆◆◆

After *Action's* English lesson, I decided that I wanted a slight break from my cave companions. But having none of the usual distractions of my normal life— television, the movies, books, the Internet, a job, social functions, exercise, hobbies, and a continuous list of things or stuff to-do—my lone and only choice was to visit another cave. I put on the rest of my wet clothes and crawled out of the cave. As I oriented myself, I sat for a moment next to the cave entrance. I was low enough in the ice that the storm didn't engulf me, but still close enough to feel the power. I was impressed, even though most of the time I desperately hated the storm because I had no control over the weather, no control over how long the storm would last, no control over anything but how my brain perceived my situation and the blizzard. And some days, I didn't have the slightest control over my brain.

I watched the wind, the ice, and the snow—awestruck at the power. The storm was not going anywhere, and unfortunately I was not going anywhere, so I might as well grow accustomed to living in it, at least for the time being. I dropped to my knees and crawled into the blizzard. *Oh God*! As soon as the freezing wind hit my wet clothing, my jacket and pants froze. Momentarily, my clothing became an ice shield, but as I moved forward, it crackled and became loose.

My knees slid across the snow; my hands prodded forward. I crawled and came to a cave entrance. I was slightly turned around, sort of lost, making me unsure whose cave I had found. Truly, it didn't matter, so I slid down the shoot.

"Yee haw!" I hooted, while sliding on my back. "Ho, ho, ho! Here comes Santa Claus!" I perched myself onto my knees.

Change, *Direction*, and *Everyday* sat Indian style on their sleeping bags. The mood was somber.

"You guys look like crap," I said, trying to be funny. It didn't work. "How's snow cave life?" I said, sarcastically, but they still didn't think I was funny.

Change looked crazy. "This is bullshit!" *Change* said as if he was alone. "Goddamn bullshit!" His eye sockets were dark.

I looked at *Direction* and *Everyday*. Their eyes told me to be patient, have some understanding, and not move too fast, like I was in the presence of a wild animal that was looking for something or someone to attack. *Nobody moves, and nobody gets hurt*!

Change grabbed his clothes bag and ripped at it, pulling and torquing it in no particular direction. "Bullshit! It's all goddamn bullshit! The storm! This mother-fucking storm! It's bullshit!"

I can relate to that, but he's gone a little crazy!

Change continued to ramble and cuss as *Direction* leaned toward me and whispered, "He does this every afternoon about four, when it's clearly apparent we're stuck for another day." As *Direction* spoke into my ear, he causally, coolly watched *Change*. "The first few days, we thought it was kinda funny, considering *Change* can be such an arrogant prick. But quickly we started feeling sorry for him."

"I feel sorry for him now!" I said, watching him rip and swear at his bag.

"Yeah, it's pretty pathetic, but unfortunately, I understand too!" *Direction* responded.

"You can say that again!" I added.

Change beat at his bag the way a boxer beats a punching bag. "No! Patagonia sucks—" His eyes swelled with tears. His lower lip flickered with frustration.

"Shouldn't we talk to him?" I asked.

"We let him get it out for about five minutes, then we ask

him questions about his life back home, and his girlfriend, Julie. Thoughts of her calm him down."

"I can't watch anymore," I said. "*Change*?" He stopped beating his bag. "Hey, tell me about your girlfriend, Julie; I hear she's a good girl!"

Change stopped abruptly, like he'd just received a shot of Demerol in the ass. He turned toward me, magically calmed. "Julie is great! I've decided that when I get back home I'm going to ask her to marry me. She's sweet and pretty, and smart, and after this crap, I'm convinced that I love her with all my heart." *Change* took in a long, deep breath and looked at his clothes bag, which he'd just finished beating with an odd expression on his face, seemingly shocked that it was in his hand. His face was one step closer to calm.

Chaos in life creates priorities.

"Yeah, Julie! Man do I love that girl! How about you guys? How's your love life?"

And so it went. A man the army had created to destroy and annihilate the enemy in foreign lands was reduced to foul language and physical acts of outrage by the winds, snow, and ice of Patagonia. *Change* was trained to withstand torture, interrogation, starvation, and enemy gunfire. But at four o'clock in the afternoon, when it was apparent we'd be bogged down for at least one more day, and travel was impossible, he could not control his emotions. He was trained, but he was not able to accept the storm for what it was—something outside of his control that he couldn't alter or change. Basically, it was just bad weather that would someday end.

February 15, 1996

My left foot itched. I was deep into my sleeping bag, and my foot was in no mans land, really, really low in the bag, but still, my foot itched. With my right foot I scraped and stabbed and poked and prodded at my left foot. Slight relief, but definitely not enough to satisfy me and stop the itch. *Maybe, just maybe, if I focus somewhere else, it'll stop the incessant itch. Mind over matter, like a Jedi with a light saber, or a monk on a mountain, or a Navy Seal with pain.*

Damn! Major itch! Screw it!

I reached for the zipper. *ZIP*! As the sleeping bag opened, the rancid smell of my rotting body violated my nostrils. My skin was like an old soggy pear in the far corner of the refrigerator. I dug my dirty fingernails into my rotting flesh. Scrape, scrape! Scrape, scrape! Ooh yeah! I raked at my foot like it was a garden. *Mind over matter! Screw that!* It was much better to scratch relief into an itch than to think it away.

I sat up. The others in the cave were either napping or thinking; both seemed boring to me. I grabbed my bag and pulled out my United States of America passport. I turned to page one. Reading material was limited and aside from the warning labels on our gear, this was the longest thing we had to read. I read the passport, cover to cover, for the tenth time.

"I need to move." I looked at the others. "Hey!" Slowly, some eyeballs turned toward me. "I need to move!"

"Go make snow angels," *Persistence* said, a suggestion so mundane, it was funny.

"I need something to do. I need something! I need to get home, I'm late!"

Persistence sat up in his sleeping bag. "Okay, you're going mental—"

"Mental!" I exclaimed.

He looked at me patiently, "Yes, mental!"

I fidgeted. *Who's he calling mental?* I twitched again. *I am fine!*

Persistence took charge. "Right now, it's time we create our mantras." He sat up; his beard appeared to be soft and groomed, nearly like a wise man's. "They can be for this moment, or if we want, for the rest of our lives! However we feel?"

Worry rolled over. "Before we philosophize and get all deep, I need to go take a poop." He slowly rubbed his head, then began to dress.

"Okay, you go squat in the hurricane, but while you're out getting in tune with nature, think of your mantra," *Persistence* said to *Worry*, winking in my direction.

Worry pulled his hood over his head, leaving only his eyes uncovered. "I assure you, while I poo, I'll be deep and meaningful." *Worry* spoke with no expression.

"Hey! This time when you shit, at least go fifty yards from the cave," I said.

"What?" *Worry* responded.

"Yeah, I'm always crawling from the cave, and boom, within five feet, I come across *Worry's* shit."

"Could roll back into the cave!" *Persistence* joked.

I was feeling a little less mental than five minutes before. "Yeah, who wants *Worry's* shit that close to home!"

"Hey! I swear, I always poo away from here; it's the wind that floats my crap over to the cave entrance." *Worry* smiled and crawled up and out.

I paused, letting *Worry* climb from the cave. "I'll give you twenty-to-one odds if we look out the cave, his bare ass is what we'll see."

Positive looked at me. "Yeah, true, but I can't blame him much. Who wants to crawl too far, and risk the wind forcing you to sit in your own crap, or worse yet, a gust of wind launching you into orbit with a cold crap hanging out your ass."

"That would sure confuse NASA," I said.

Persistence put his hand to his mouth, speaking like a mundane radio controller for NASA. "We have an unidentified mountaineer, entering the earth's atmosphere—hold on, he has frozen shit hanging out his ass! Call the president. We're under attack by hairy, smelly mountaineers, and they've got laser-guided shit missiles."

I chuckled painfully. "Oh man, what's my life become?"

After five minutes, *Worry* rolled back down the snow cave entrance. He bounced into the cave, rolled to one side, and sat back up. He smiled. "Light as a feather. And, while I was out, I thought of my mantra. You guys got yours?"

"Got mine!"

"Yep."

"Okay—"

Suddenly and surprisingly, *Action*, *Slack*, and *Positive* came sliding down into the small cave.

"Hey, I hear it's party time at your place!" *Positive* said.

Every inch of space in the cave was filled by a foot, a shoulder, an arm, or a leg.

Slack continued to lighten the mood. "Yeah, I was out in the blizzard for a casual stroll, and I ran into this other frozen ass. I said hello, but its mouth was full—"

"Always best to let shit fly in the safety of friends— " *Worry* interrupted.

Good point, I thought.

"Someone needs to hold your ass to earth," continued *Worry*. "So after I let it all hang out, I told them to come to our place for a little bonfire on the beach, some cold beer, and weenie roasting."

"My weenie hasn't been roasted for weeks!" *Persistence* laughed.

"Mine could use some roasting!" *Worry* exclaimed with a huge smile.

"I haven't even seen my weenie since I stepped foot into Patagonia!" I added.

"I'd kill for a warm place to warm my weenie!" *Positive* howled.

A roar of laugher erupted. Cock talk! We hadn't mentioned our penises for weeks; it had been days and days since we had engaged in useless male banter. It was familiar, it was comfortable, it was juvenile, and God bless, it made our situation more human and bearable.

And while the group laughed, I realized I had not had a sexual thought for weeks. Not one! No visions of female breasts or bottoms, no dreams or desires. No random, wondering, uncontrollable erections. I was void of sexual desire. *Wow,* I thought. *I have to be on the verge of death, but yes, it is possible that survival does override sex. Amazing!*

Persistence interrupted my thoughts. "The question to the

group: What's your mantra for this trek? Or better yet, what's your new mantra for life?"

Worry got excited. "I got mine. It's simple—"

"Let's hear it," *Persistence* said.

Everybody settled back, packed extremely tight into the snow cave. For a short time, we forgot our walls were ice.

"Don't poo where you sleep!" *Worry* exclaimed.

"What?" *Slack* said. "That's your mantra?"

"Yeah. Seriously, don't poo where you sleep. Like don't have random sex with people at the office, or no screwing a roommate, and especially don't hump people who live in your apartment building—"

"No pulling a Melrose Place," *Persistence* added.

Worry continued. "Yeah. Better to go jogging in the hills than to run off at the mouth at work. And especially, don't tell your in-laws what you really think of their political views during the first couple of Thanksgiving dinners. Just don't crap where you sleep cause it may get in your hair, and nobody looks good with shit in their hair!"

The cave clamored with clapping hands and various hoots and howls.

"Hear, hear!" we joked.

"Put me another weenie on the roaster!" *Persistence* shouted.

"Pass me beer!" *Slack* said.

"Hey! Who was supposed to bring the women?" I added.

"Who's next?" *Persistence* asked.

There was a brief pause before *Persistence* began with his mantra. "I'll go!" He rubbed his hands together. "Pull the covers off your desire!"

"You mean like go after your dreams?"

"Better to do it than continue to dream it!"

"Don't let life pass you by!"

Persistence interjected: "You bet, all of those, and I'll expand. Desire is for those who don't get out of bed in the morning. People who always talk about what they are going to do in life, and then never do a damn thing! Desire points you in the right direction, but for Christ's sake, pull the covers off your desire. Go after what you want!"

"I like that," I said.

"I'll go!" *Slack* said. He was more excited than I'd ever seen him. He used his hands as he spoke. "God said, 'Be brief!' "

"You mean like die quick?" *Persistence* asked.

"Nope! I mean people always complicate life, bend their lives when they don't need to." *Slack's* hands moved side to side as he spoke. "They take simple and make it complicated!"

Persistence interjected: "Like religion. Numerous cultures have been creating books, and groups, and wars, and conflict for centuries. It's such crap! All religious groups should be summed up in one word: love! No more, no less! The rest is just horseshit!"

"He's got it!" *Slack* said.

"Who's next?" *Persistence* asked.

"My mantra's not new," *Positive* said.

"Let's hear it," I said.

"Get busy living!" *Positive* said intensely.

"That's brief," *Slack* commented.

"Simple!" I said.

"I'm a simple guy." *Positive* looked around the cave.

"You mean like get busy living, or get busy dying?" *Persistence* asked.

"No, not that." *Positive* said, somewhat offended. "That gives a person an out, an excuse to not grab life by the balls and drain the good stuff! I mean: Get busy living! Period! Exclamation point! There shouldn't be any other option in life. Get busy living!"

"Drain the good stuff out of whose balls! Ouch!"

I smiled. "Back to my previous question—how come no one brought women to this party?"

"Me!" *Action* said like a true Spanish speaker. "My time!"

"Let's hear it, *Action*!"

"Steeper it get, more it hurt, better it feel!" *Action* smiled, pleased with his English.

There was a pause as we silently translated the broken English to its true meaning.

"Can I clean that up a little?" *Persistence* asked.

Action nodded his approval.

"The steeper it gets, the more it hurts, the better it feels." *Persistence* looked at *Action*.

He smiled. "¡Sí! That!"

"Easy to understand in the mountains," *Worry* said.

"He's talking about much more than just the mountains; he's talking about life." *Positive* pointed toward *Action*, as if to say, *You sneaky little dog you!* "All things in life that are worth attaining are worth working for, worth some pain, worth some sweat, worth climbing a hill. Because in the end, when the sun sets, the reward of getting what you want justifies the pain of getting to the top!"

Action winked at *Positive*. He didn't understand all the English words, but he had watched *Positive* for weeks and *Action* knew he understood.

"Okay, you're last," *Persistence* said, looking at me.

"I thought of this the other day when I was full of pain, pulling one of those lazy ass pigs!" I said.

"It's a sled!" someone interjected.

"Oh, it's much more than a sled. It's life weighing you down, pulling you backward!"

"This ought to be good!" *Positive* said, smiling. "What is it?"

"One life—make your move." I said. The cave grew silent. I looked around. Didn't they understand me? So once again, I said, "One life—make your move."

More silence, too much silence and then I realized. As a group, we were stuck in snow caves on the Northern Patagonian Ice Field because we had made a move. Death was near because we had grabbed life by the neck. We were slowly starving because we decided to climb that mountain. The silence could have been ten seconds, or ten minutes, but slowly our faces changed and we came to grips with our various choices.

"Better to live and then die!"

"One life!"

"Better than watching fucking TV!"

"What doesn't kill you only makes you stronger!"

"One life—make that move!"

Do we believe this stuff? I don't truly know. Would I come to Patagonia again, or repeat this trip, if I could know the future? Not sure. If I don't die, and live more life in the years to come, then yes, of course. If I die, then probably no! Regardless: One life—make your move!

February 16, 1996

Persistence cooked breakfast for *Worry* and me. The prior night, the group had decided to follow a strong suggestion from *Direction* that we begin to ration our food. So we each ate one handful of oatmeal mixed with butter and sugar, all covered with instant milk. I was grateful to be eating.

Worry sat up on his knees. "I'll be back. I want to see if I can borrow the *Outdoor Cook Book* from *Direction*; I need something to read this afternoon," *Worry* said.

"Don't be gone long, honey!" I said.

"Hey, see if you can rent some snowmobiles while you're out," *Persistence* joked.

I laughed. Anything remotely funny was very funny in a snow cave.

"*Today*, you start cleaning up breakfast, and when I get back I'll finish the job," *Worry* said.

"Sounds good," I answered.

There was not a lot to clean up, but we had gotten used to more pots, pans, and utensils. Prior to rationing the food and fuel, our normal breakfast would have been three handfuls of oatmeal, a few cups of hot chocolate, and maybe three of four pancakes. We had decided that hot chocolate was a waste of stove fuel and that completely boiling water was not necessary, so we'd just melt the ice into water and never heat the water past lukewarm.

We had just cut our calorie intake by seventy-five percent, but at the same time, we were not hiking, or pulling hundreds of pounds with our bodies. The calories had one purpose: to keep us warm, to keep us alive.

I finished cleaning the pots and bowls. It took no time at all, and the fact that *Worry* had not returned promptly to clean his portion of breakfast was not an issue. I turned my attention to the ceiling. The morning was good. I had a calm about me. After some time, I passed into a light sleep.

◆◆◆

I opened my eyes. The cave was quiet. I sat up to my butt and removed my socks. My feet were cold. I rubbed my eyes with my pasty, soggy hands. I could feel my skin mush together. *I am slowly rotting!*

Persistence opened his eyes. "How long we been napping?" he asked.

"Not sure. What time is it?" I asked.

"My watch's in my jacket, I got tired of looking at the time every two hours. Where's your watch?"

"I gave it to *Worry* yesterday so he could time his heartbeat. He was trying to see how slow he could get his heart rate," I said.

"Where the hell is *Worry*?" *Persistence* asked.

"Not sure; he probably came back to the cave and didn't feel like watching us nap and went to one of the other caves. So pull your watch out; I want to know how long until we can make dinner."

"Okay." *Persistence* began to shuffle in his gear. "Give me a minute."

We had two high points in each day—breakfast and dinner, our two meals. The two or three naps in between the two meals were nice. Sleeping and eating helped us forget that we were slowly starving and rotting. Each day dinner grew slightly closer to the lunch hour, but we forced ourselves to delay as long as possible because the later we ate our dinner, the warmer we'd sleep with the fresh calories generating heat for our bodies.

"Here it is!" *Persistence* said as he pulled his watch from a jacket pocket. "Wow! We slept a while; it's nearly one."

"Wow, that was a long nap. What time did we eat this morning?" I asked.

"What, about nine, nine thirty."

"That's what I'd guess," I said as I grabbed the water bottle and took a deep swig. It was odd—the entire cave was damp and moist, but my mouth was bone dry. The water quickly cured my cottonmouth.

"Hey, you see that cookbook *Worry* was reading?" *Persistence* asked.

I shuffled through *Worry's* bag and gear. "Not here," I said.

"I wonder if he returned the thing already."

"Couldn't tell you," I answered.

Persistence began to shuffle around and put his thick plastic mountaineering boots on his feet. "I'll be back. I'm going to get some reading material," he said.

"The cookbook?" I asked.

"Yep. You need anything from *Direction's* cave?"

"Nope."

Persistence disappeared, up and out, into the storm and off to one of the other caves. I looked around. It was silent. I realized that for more than a week, in the chaos of the storm I had either been fighting for my life or spending time with the other men in one of the caves or tents. Now I was alone. It was eerie. And instantly and suddenly I was overcome with two separate and drastically different emotions. I was very, very happy to have other people with me during this storm, this time of trial in my life. Contrasting that thought, I was very troubled by the loneliness of the cave at that exact moment. I was alone in the storm, and at the same time, I was struggling with many others.

What a dichotomy. Always alone and never alone at the same time!

I continued to look around my cave. It wasn't that bad. Then, as suddenly as my realization came, it vanished as *Persistence* came rolling down the snow cave chute. He lay there on his side, looking nervously back and forth.

"What?" I asked, as his eyes jerked side to side.

"You seen *Worry*?"

"Nope."

"Oh fuck!" *Persistence's* eyes filled with fear. "He never made it to *Direction's* cave this morning to get the cookbook. He hasn't been seen for hours by anyone!"

"What!"

"You heard me—he's gone!"

"What!"

"Put your crap on! Meet me in *Direction's* cave!"

As I dressed, my heartbeat increased. My hands began to shake. I couldn't imagine being lost in the storm. Fear took hold as I crawled from my shelter into the blizzard. Instantly, the wind forced me to the ground. Patagonia was raging. I hadn't been on the surface in nearly twenty-four hours. The storm was fierce and vicious. The pit we had built all the caves in was filling with fresh powder. The wind swirled the snow into miniature but violent little cyclones, uncontrollable circles of power.

I oriented myself. The blasting power of the storm had increased to epic proportions. *Direction*, *Change*, *Everyday*, and *Persistence* crawled from another cave. They were in full blizzard gear. *Change* had his headlamp on his head, which also held his jacket and hat firmly to his head. *Direction* and *Everyday* held three ropes. *Persistence* was holding ice screws and snow pickets. I adjusted my clothes, ready to search.

We were huddled close as *Action*, *Slack*, and *Positive* joined the huddle from their cave.

"*Worry* is gone!" *Direction* said. "And they're only two options! Either *Worry* got lost, or the wind took him! Either way, he's out there, possibly stuck in a crevasse, maybe just lying on the open ice! At this point, he's been gone for at least two or three hours. He could be covered in snow. Could be unconscious!"

I forced myself to slow my breathing, but I was filled with fear.

I am alive in this moment. Nothing else on earth exists. Chaos has given new life and new power to Cowboy Now. This is my moment to conquer fear!

I took the longest, slowest, most deliberate breath into my lungs that I had ever experienced!

Direction continued speaking and I listened. "This is what we're doing! We'll separate into teams of two, us four separate teams. The snow pit is center of our search grid. We'll secure three separate anchor points and one team won't be roped in, ready for any emergency backup needs. The team that's off the rope will have one person in a cave, boiling water, lots of water, for *Worry* once we find him. Second person on the team that's boiling water will stand at the cave's entrance, so that the three people on the rope anchors can communicate emergency needs. We'll rope up, and three people wide, we'll walk away from the snow pit, shoulder to shoulder, for a full rope length. The other three on the anchors will feed rope as they walk away from the pit. Once the rope is fully extended, the three on the end of the ropes will sidestep clockwise and return, just like mowing a lawn, covering every inch. Once back at the anchors, we'll repeat the process until we cover every part of the search grid."

Direction handed me a rope. "Any questions?" He didn't wait long enough for anyone to think about or doubt his plan. "Good! *Today*, you and *Persistence. Positive*, you and *Slack. Everyday*, you and *Action. Change*, you're with me! *Everyday*, you and *Action* start boiling the water. Everyone, check your ropes twice, check your harnesses twice, then check each other!"

As I prepared the ropes and snow anchors, I thought. In my life, the only thing that compared with the pressure I felt from this crazy fiasco took place years earlier on the final play of a championship high school football. No time on the clock, one last play with the game on the line. One moment we were in a huddle, with separate thoughts and ideas about the outcome: There could've been success, failure, joy, or misery. If we won, celebration; if we lost, tears. The play got diagrammed and we broke the huddle, moving in separate directions, but toward the same common goal. We all knew the plan and the play, and at the same time we all had different jobs to do, but at the root of the play, we had one common goal: to succeed! Years ago, in football, our goal was victory, glory, and the payoff of months of hard and diligent work. In Patagonia, our goal was life. Totally different, and yet completely identical.

Preparation is the same, whether it's for victory or for life.

Everyone was in place. The ice screws and snow pickets were secured. The ropes were ready. Attached to the safety anchors were *Change*, *Slack*, and *Persistence*. Connected to the ropes and the first wave of the search were *Direction*, *Positive*, and I. The three of us stood side by side, roped to three separate people, on three separate anchors.

Into the white we walked. I carried my ice axe in my right hand. Within feet, I was thrown sideways into *Positive*. He fell to his left and knocked *Direction* to the ice. The three of us lay in one big pile of legs, arms, and rope.

Damn it!

"Dominoes!" *Positive* screamed into the wind.

"That was interesting. Watch your ice axes!" *Direction* yelled.

I looked down to *Positive*, his right eye squeezed out a wink. We unpiled to our knees. We had only walked ten feet, and behind us, we couldn't see *Change*, *Slack*, or *Persistence*. The entire world was white.

As we cautiously stood, *Positive* locked into my arm at my elbow. I looked over to my left and saw he'd also secured himself tightly to *Direction's* arm.

Now we're just one big kite.

We leaned forward, pointing our heads into the roaring wind. Our steps were short, quick, and secure. We had three goals— walk straight, pay attention, and find *Worry*. I felt like I could not see any more than six inches into the distance, but was unsure since I was engulfed by white. The ice mixing with the wind made it impossible to look forward, forcing me to focus on the ground.

The ropes were one hundred and fifty feet long. We were at the end of our ropes, and nothing! Not a single sign of anything except the white stew of Patagonia.

We turned back toward the snow pit, lifted the ropes back over our heads, and then slid four feet to the left. With

Direction an inch from the footprints I had made walking away from the pit, we started back, this time at a little faster pace, with the wind at our backs. My eyes worked, scouring every inch of snow, looking for anything but the white. Unexpectedly, the wind shifted and lifted us into the air, throwing us five feet forward. We landed on our feet. We all looked at one another. I was shocked to still be standing. *Positive* smirked slightly.

We attempted to take small steps, but the wind pushed hard, increasing our stride. Back at the snow pit, the three anchor men were getting cold. They just sat, holding the ropes we were connected to, getting pushed and tossed like rag dolls, slowly growing colder.

We spun away from the snow pit and walked back into the white abyss. As I walked my legs forward, my nose grew cold. My feet labored to find balance, and I continued to pull tighter upon *Positive's* arm. The wind blasted. The three of us fell backward to our butts. I looked over at the two leaders. No emotion. This was search and rescue, not *Alice in Wonderland*. We stumbled to our feet, again locked arms, and moved farther into the storm. My cheeks began to feel frozen. I struggled to stay focused.

Two hours passed. We had repeated the process, over and over, creating a full circle. *Change*, *Slack*, and *Persistence* were quiet, all three nursing a fresh batch of hot chocolate. They had been crouching by the snow pit, attempting to stay warm, but slowly losing heat and energy.

"Who needs a break?" *Direction* looked us over. "Anyone?"

We all needed a break, including *Direction*, but we had no time or energy to spare.

"You three, it's your turn; we need to go around one more time, make sure we didn't miss him on our first sweep." *Direction* spoke with an authority I had never witnessed;

then again, I had never been searching for a man's life.

Change, *Slack*, and *Persistence* untied from the snow anchors. *Direction*, *Positive* and I tied into the snow anchors. With doubt in their eyes, they left the pit, and ventured into the white. I fed rope as *Persistence* walked away from me. After ten minutes, there was no more rope, and as it grew tight, there was a brief pause before *Persistence* and the rope began moving back toward me. Another ten minutes, and the group of three, locked arm in arm, emerged from the white. Their faces showed fear. I tried to smile, or wink, or chat, or do something in the general direction of the three men searching, but my face did not respond. I was petrified! The three turned away and struggled back into the white.

I sat huddled over myself. I was alone, even with two men directly next to me. I was a fixture in the snow, a bump on a log, a mountain, a dying tree, a coastline. I was being weathered, stripped of my texture and energy. The wind continued, the snow fell, and bit-by-bit, I was losing. I buried my head deeper into my jacket.

Christ, I am freezing to death! God help me! Too young to die!

A sudden tap on my shoulder startled me. At first, I was confused, and then I looked up. *Action* stood above me.

"Here. Drink." He handed me a water bottle full of the hottest, thickest hot chocolate any man had ever created.

I grabbed the bottle. "Tihnku." I tried to speak, but my words were frozen to my tongue. He looked at me curiously. Again I tried to speak. "Tihnku!"

Screw it! Nothing was right. *Action* vanished. I drank the hot chocolate.

Another two hours passed. *Change*, *Slack*, and *Persistence* had finished their sweep without a single sighting of anything but snow and ice.

The group gathered.

"Who needs a break?" Direction looked us over. "Anyone?"

God yes, we need a break! We're killing ourselves! In another five minutes, what good will we be! I was too cold to speak, or argue, or doubt.

"One more time we go round, this time we go two rope lengths out! Let's move before we get cold!" *Direction* said, still confident.

Who's he bullshitting? I'm freezing! This is way past cold.

Every part of me wanted to stop, but I kept moving. *Direction*, *Positive*, and I unhooked from the snow anchors. I looked into *Direction's* blue face. He was frozen but not cold. He had one priority: finding *Worry*, and finding *Worry* alive.

I was tired. I was cold. I was miserable. But one more time I walked into the white hell of Patagonia. I walked like a zombie, ten feet, twenty feet, thirty feet, forty feet, fifty feet, sixty feet, seventy feet, eighty feet, ninety feet. I stopped when the rope stopped.

Too young to die! Too young to die! Too young to die! Too young to die! Over and over in my head, like a song. I put a beat to it. *Too young to die! Too young to die! Too young to die! Too young to die!*

Back at the anchors *Change*, *Slack*, and *Persistence* added a second rope to our search line. An additional hundred feet of rope, and we moved forward. One hundred feet. One hundred and ten feet. One hundred and thirty feet. I was walking myself to death. There was no question!

Today is dying!

I stopped, which forced *Direction* and *Positive* to stop too.

I am freezing to death because some asshole can't help himself. Screw him! Let him die! I am done killing Today in search of Worry.

I turned weakly to *Positive* and *Direction*. "He's gone! He's fucking dead!" I mumbled, my energy nearly lost. "And if we keep looking, we're going to goddamn join him!"

There, I think I made my point!

Direction grabbed my shoulder hard, and squeezed. "Listen, you selfish little prick! Would you want us to stop looking if you were lost, if you were alone! Would you?" His eyes raged.

As he spoke, I heard his anger, his words, his disgust at my lack of compassion, but then his voice became blurred as my mind caught a color. In that universe of white, I thought I spied a subtle star of black. I refocused. My eyes saw something. Or was I too tired? Again I refocused and quickly stepped to my right and forward. More black! It was a jacket. It was *Worry*!

"HEY!" I tried to run to him, but the rope pulled tight. I pulled hard for slack. "JESUS CHRIST!" I scampered desperately to him.

Face-down in the ice, mostly covered in snow, lay *Worry's* still and frozen body. I dropped to my knees. "Jesus Christ!" As I hit the ice, *Direction* and *Positive* arrived by my side. "HEY!" I attempted to roll *Worry's* body. A leg and foot were wedged tight into a crevasse. I ripped my jacket from my body, lifted his head and placed the jacket on the ice under his face. I turned his head toward me. He was blue. He was frosted. He was silent and still.

"I think he's dead." My body felt numb. "I think he's fucking dead!" I screamed.

Direction dropped to his knees at my left. "He's not dead until I say he's dead."

"He's gone." My body sank.

"Move!" *Direction* pushed me to the left.

Positive wasn't paying attention to anything above his waist; he had begun working to free *Worry's* leg and foot.

Guilt flushed my body. *Worry* was human. *Worry* was as human as every single human on earth. He was born to this earth, and he would die on this earth. *Worry* was human.

"Hey!" I screamed at *Worry*.

I looked at *Positive*, then at *Direction*. I rolled to my hip.

Goddamn it! Worry was human!

At that moment, *Direction* was like a god. On his knees, he slid closer to *Worry*, removed his gloves, and cradled *Worry's* head. My hip sank deeper into the ice. I was paralyzed. *Direction* and *Positive* had forgotten the storm. *Direction* placed his cheek to the mouth of *Worry* and grabbed hold of his neck.

My hip sank deeper into the ice. I could not move.

"Got it! I got a faint pulse!" *Direction* yelled.

"What?" I drooled from my mouth.

Positive hadn't stopped to consider whether *Worry* was dead or alive; he continued to work to free his trapped leg.

"He what?" I said again.

Direction spoke to me without looking at me. "*Today*, go get a sleeping bag. Fill it with as many hot water bottles as we've got. Do it now!

Like a robot, I stood; this was no longer my life. Nor was this about my survival. I moved rapidly. Twice, I was thrown to the ice by the wind, and oddly, each time I didn't care. I crawled, and pushed, and scrambled my way back to the snow pit.

"We got him. He's alive. Barely, but he's alive," I said.

"God help us!"

I dropped into the snow pit. The sleeping bag was ready

with five bottles of warm water. Quickly, I crawled back into the storm as the wind pulled at the sleeping bag like it was a sail. My body followed and I fell to my knees. "Dammit!" I wrapped my arms tighter around the bag. I stood and was thrown sideways, but stayed vertical this time. I walked, my head pointed into the wind, focusing only on the two ropes at my feet that would lead me to the others.

When I reached them, I found that *Positive* had freed both *Worry's* legs and was checking for any broken bones in his lower body. *Direction* was straddling *Worry's* upper torso, with both hands to his cheeks.

"No broken bones, or none I can find," *Positive* said.

"Good, then we move him now," *Direction* said.

I fell to my knees.

"Unzip the bag, hold it tight, and pile the water bottles just there. Now that his legs are free, we won't use the water until we get him back to a cave," *Direction* said.

I made a fast pile of water bottles by my feet and unzipped the bag.

"*Positive*, hold that end still." *Direction* was in charge of everything; it almost seemed as if he could control the storm.

To the right of *Worry's* frozen, nearly stiff body, we laid the sleeping bag. I held the top; *Positive* held the bottom. *Direction* pulled the limp body into the bag.

"Zip him in."

Positive jumped forward and secured the sleeping bag at the top. After that, he looped a piece of rope around the sleeping bag and around *Worry's* shins. He cinched it tight, and we were ready to pull *Worry* back to the cave. "Ready to roll," he said.

Direction tilted his head and looked sideways at me.

"Here. Take our ice axes. Put the water bottles in this bag." He handed me a small bag. "You walk just behind us as we take him back to the caves."

I stood. And as I did, the wind took my wool hat right off my head. My hands were full, so I couldn't grab for it, or even look to see where it went. I knew it was long gone. It belonged to the storm. Instantly, my head was cold. I didn't care as I looked down at the still, blue face of *Worry*.

Positive lifted *Worry's* legs; both were surrounded and secured in the sleeping bag. He began to walk backward. *Direction* followed, staying nearly on top of *Worry's* head. I stayed focused to keep two paces behind.

The wind roared and seared our bodies with waves of ice and snow. For the first time, we walked in a straight line. *Positive*, *Worry*, *Direction*, and I all had one goal; it was life, and it trumped everything else. We walked a straight line back to the snow pit.

Positive pulled *Worry* around to the other side of the pit, to the top of the snow ramp, and slid him down toward the cave's entrance. *Everyday's* head was peering out of the cave like a trapdoor spider. In one swift motion, he pulled *Worry* into the cave. *Direction* and *Positive* went into the cave.

Change, *Slack*, and *Persistence* had detached themselves from the snow anchors and joined *Action* and me at the bottom of the snow pit. In a circle we stood in silence.

Life is precious! Life is gold!

After two minutes, *Direction* crawled from the cave.

"Here's what we're going to do. *Everyday* has all four stoves burning; he's making warm water and warm food. The rest of us need to generate heat. So we work and shovel. After our bodies are nice and warm, one by one, we'll go into the cave, eat some warm food, drink warm water, strip totally naked while our bodies are generating the maximum amount of heat, and cover *Worry* in a naked human blanket of warmth."

Not a word was said among any of us heterosexual males.

Life is precious! Life is gold!

Direction continued. "Once your body is done generating maximum heat, you'll put your clothes back on and someone else who's been eating and drinking will strip naked and climb in the bag with *Worry*. The other person will climb out of the cave and begin to generate more heat."

"Is he going to live?" someone asked. I'm not sure who—it could've been me.

"Of course!" *Direction* was confident. He was leading. "We may have to do this for hours, maybe for a day, maybe two. You'd better think about who you all are as humans. This may get very, very tiring."

Again, not a word was said among any of us tired, frozen, heterosexual males.

Life is precious! Life is gold!

"I will stay by his side until his eyes open." *Direction* turned toward me. "*Today*, make sure you dismantle those rope anchors before the storm covers the pickets and ice screws." He turned and went back into the cave.

Persistence, *Slack*, *Change*, and *Action* all grabbed shovels.

"*Slack*, we'll generate heat right now," *Persistence* said. "*Change*, you and *Action* pace yourself until we disappear into the cave."

I crawled out of the snow pit and walked to the snow anchors. My mind was silent. I had a common goal, a common direction. As I dismantled the snow anchors, I once again reflected back upon my high school football experience. My hands worked as I drew from my past experience.

We'd won the high school football game with no time on

the clock. It was splendid! It was glorious! It was heroic! It taught me about working with others for a common goal. It taught me to sacrifice self for a common good. But never in a million years would I have thought it would prepare me to strip naked and climb into a wet, moldy, smelly sleeping bag with another man. How far would I go to save another human's life? I would sacrifice self until death. We had a common goal, and it was life.

Life is precious! Life is gold!

February 17, 1996

Worry opened an eye. It had been twenty-four hours since we pulled him from the ice, nearly dead. *Direction* turned to me and smiled. *Everyday* was leaning against the ice wall; he grinned. Both *Everyday* and *Direction* hadn't slept in two days. *Worry's* other eye opened. Twenty-four hours straight, we had continuously covered *Worry* in a blanket of human warmth. His eyes looked around the cave. A faint but slight smile appeared on his face.

Direction poured a small amount of water into a bottle lid. "Welcome back," he said. "You want water?"

Worry nodded yes. *Direction* dripped water into his mouth.

"I'm not dead?" *Worry* said.

"You're not dead." *Direction* responded.

Worry smiled, a little larger than the first time. "I'm not dead." His eyes closed.

"You rest. You're okay now." *Direction* said.

As *Worry* fell into a deep sleep, I knew my respect and trust for *Direction* had multiplied. Eight men, grappling and fighting for only the grimmest survival and any trace of hope that tomorrow the sun would return, had saved the life of another man.

It is amazing what the warmth of man will do for a cold human!

February 19, 1996

My mother sat on a green couch, a bag of popcorn in one hand. She was staring happily and peacefully at the television. The air was warm, dry, and comfortable. My skin was happy. I could hear the crackle of a great homemade fire in the wood-burning stove. I could smell the drab, beige carpet that adorned the home of my youth. My mother chewed rhythmically and peacefully on her popcorn. She smiled at me. I smiled back. I was happy.

I understood that I was only dreaming. I also understood that I didn't want to wake up from the dream. Dreams had become the way I connected my cave with my home back in America. I was also learning that my dreams were a road map for where I wanted to go in life. What I would dream about at night was what I wanted. Now, my dreams were about comfort and food. And conversely, my nightmares signaled the caution signs on my current path of life, warning me of my fears and pitfalls. My dear mother began to fade.

I want my mother!

Damn! My body shivered. The cold and wet were calling my name. My temporary sleep was over. My eyes cranked open. I leaned forward in my sleeping bag and tried to focus in the darkness. Nothing! I was obviously still in the cave and not with my mother.

I shivered and my wet skin crawled. I rubbed my eye sockets, attempting to focus, but my hands slipped over my eyes. My face was too wet. I looked around for something to dry my face. My jacket was wet, my hands were wet, my hat was wet, my gloves were wet, and my long underwear was wet. Again, I rubbed my face. And again, my hands sloshed over my skin.

I pulled my clothes from the various enclaves of my shelter. I dressed myself in wet, cold, dreary clothing. The cave was just cold enough to keep the clothes wet and not frozen, but unfortunately much too cold to dry anything. I put my pants, jacket, hood, and gloves on my wet body. They clung heavily to my frame.

I crawled out of the cave, through the tight snow passageway between cave and storm. I slithered to the top of the cave entrance; it was covered by two feet of fresh snow. I pointed my head and pushed it into the snow. The ice raked at my face. Instantly, I was awake, finding it hard to be tired in gale-force winds.

As much as I hated living underground, living in the ice, slowly starving and freezing, a bizarre, sluggish comfort had begun to settle upon me. The cave was familiar. The storm was not. I stood, and saw that to my right *Change* was clearing the entrance to one of the other caves. He shoveled, up and down, heaving snow over his left shoulder. *Change* was a large, broad-shouldered man. His physical motion was powerful.

There was a constant flow of wind and ice. The hiss of the wind was overwhelming. I imagined that a similar feeling would be to stand behind the jet engine of a 747 aircraft, as small pebbles were fed into the engine. Little ice bullets attacked my face and body.

"HEY!" I yelled to *Change*. Nothing! He continued to shovel. "*Change*!" I screamed, straining my vocal cords to their limit.

I walked toward him and stood directly to his right. He took two more shovel strokes, then noticed my feet and stopped working. He thrust the shovel into the snow, looked at me, and smiled.

Hmm! Curious. I didn't know this man knew how to smile.

I shook my head and looked again at *Change*. His face was happy, pleasant. "What are you smiling at?" I asked, an inch from his ear.

He continued to smile, as if he was being sarcastic, but he wasn't. After a long, happy pause, he moved close to me.

I allowed *Change* to move close to me.

"Life is good!" he said, inches from my ear, then regained eye contact with me.

Life is good? Change could be drastic, Change could be cruel, Change could be powerful, but up until now, I had never thought of Change as happy!

Change's smile grew, then he gave me a nod and went straight back to shoveling. For a brief moment, I wondered if *Change* had gone insane. But as I watched *Change* pick up his shovel again, I noticed he was moving to a lighter rhythm, a more peaceful pace. Besides, it wasn't as if we could've taken him to a psychiatrist. And if he was insane, he was by far more pleasant this way.

Change isn't a dick! Maybe Change is just a little crazy sometimes.

I began to shovel the entrance to my cave. The wind was loud, but my mind was silent. Every ten or twenty shovel strokes, I'd glance toward *Change*, and he was still happy.

At that point, I stopped worrying about *Change*.

An hour passed, maybe two, possibly three, but it didn't matter, it was still dark and the wind still blew. I had successfully cleared a snow path to the entrance of my cave.

Change was evolving. He stood entranced, gazing into the sky. I followed his look. Ah yes! Beauty! For the first time in weeks, I could see cloud formations in the sky. There wasn't a single indication of a star, and the clouds were still dark, deep, and ugly. But instead of a conglomeration of pure gray, where all the clouds formed one drab, colossus of a night sky and the world was lost, there were dark, mean-looking clouds. It was beautiful.

"That's great," *Change* said.

I looked down. He had moved close to me as he happily bobbed his head.

"Yep. Who would've ever thought that dark, gray, gloomy clouds in the middle of the night could be so beautiful?" I said.

"Seems peaceful tonight," he said, his eyes relaxed.

"You seem peaceful tonight," I answered.

"Yeah." He said it slowly and calmly, like Dustin Hoffman in Rainman.

"What gives?"

"The night's good. I'm alive," he responded.

"You're most definitely alive; the night's questionable." But he was right about both; he was alive, and the night was oddly pleasant. I looked back at the sky.

The clouds drifted through and into one another. They mixed, then separated, and then mixed again. Some moved slightly faster, while others seemed to hang on their tips, no motion. Big ones, small ones, fat ones, thin ones. Dark black, deep blue, and hazy purple.

"Amazing!" I said.

"You want some water?" *Change* offered his water bottle to me.

"Thank you." I took a big gulp of the water.

Oddly enough, this was the first time *Change* had ever offered or given me anything since I had met him weeks earlier.

"Okay! What's up?"

He smiled at me. "Nothing!"

I glared at him sarcastically, as if to say, *Where's the dick in you gone?* He understood. He had always been a dick, not dumb.

"Well, after watching *Worry* nearly die, and all the help you guys have given to me, and all this forced self-examination—it's just different now!"

I understood. And *Change* knew I understood, so no more words were needed.

"I've always been bigger, better, stronger, smarter, at everything. And I just never thought it was a big deal that I was arrogant. I was better, so I figured, who cares?" The tone in his voice was soft. His demeanor was humble.

"Don't tell me you've had some deep, inspirational experience—" I was about to tell him I was joking when he interrupted.

"No! Not that! But my father has this quote on his desk at work, something like: When the chess game is over, the king and pawn go back in the same box. And I never got it until now."

"I like that!" I said, my head cranked toward the sky, gazing straight into the black night.

"Yeah, because really, when the game of life is over, the rock star and the janitor go back into the same soil." *Change* paused, but only briefly. "Death is life's greatest equalizer!"

◆◆◆

The days had begun to blur. One day seemed like the last, and tomorrow seemed to have a guarantee attached to it: We would be living in an ice cave. Hours and hours and hours and hours would pass in silence. But after a while, it was the simple things that forced our interaction.

"Pass the piss bottle please," *Change* said.

Worry reached to his left, shuffled through some wet, soggy gear, and grabbed a bottle nearly full of urine. Since the start of the storm, we had been using a water bottle for urination. This made it easier and more convenient to pee without having to crawl to the surface. When the bottle filled, we'd pour it in the far corner of the cave. It would freeze, leaving no smell, just a yellow hole that grew larger by the day.

"Here." *Worry* handed *Change* a bottle full of urine.

The moisture in the air was thick. The faint glow of sun was barely adequate. I rubbed my hands together, attempting to generate heat to dry my wet skin. "I've been having dreams of McDonald's," I said, gyrating my hands against each other.

"Aren't you a vegetarian?" *Persistence* asked.

"Yep! But I'm also human, and humans don't live like this. Last night I dreamt about piles and piles of greasy fries, Big Macs, chocolate shakes—the works!" I added.

"Now that's my kind of dream," *Change* said, as he began to shuffle around his sleeping bag with his various zippers and Velcro straps. Under his bag, he turned his butt into the air and began to piss.

Trickle, trickle, trickle.

"Oh the splendid glory of mountaineering," *Persistence* said as he watched *Change* urinate.

"Don't mind me; keep on with your food stories," *Change* said seriously.

"My father told me a story once that relates to my Big Mac

dreams," I said, as I glanced obviously at my watch. "You guys got a minute for a story?"

"That's not funny," *Worry* droned, while picking at his teeth.

I smiled; snow cave humor was an art. "My father had this business acquaintance. Rich, rich, rich man. One of those estate owners. Four-, five-, six-car garage— something like that. The guy collected art. Real expensive art. And one day, he had a handful of Japanese businessmen to his home for a meeting. As he was giving them a tour of his personal castle, they happened upon his art collection. As they walked down the line of expensive art, consisting of only the best of Van Gogh, Matisse, Picasso, and so forth, the oldest Japanese man, who was a billionaire, wanted to know the cost of the art, so he boldly asked, 'How much does that one cost?,' pointing to an original Picasso. Calmly, the owner stated, 'That one is around a million dollars.' Proudly he added, 'About an average price for the pieces in my collection.'

"As the group moved forward examining the world-famous art, once again the eldest Japanese man stopped in front of a piece of art. He said, 'This one looks more modern, with all these fancy colors blended perfectly, reds, pinks, yellows, greens. This one, I want to buy. How much?' 'Oh, that one there is priceless, and not for sale,' came the reply. The Japanese billionaire smiled proudly, and said, 'All things are for sale; I like this, and will give you one million dollars for it.' The businessman smiled humbly, and said, 'I thank you, but as I said, that one is not for sale.' The Japanese billionaire looked at it once more, and then proclaimed, 'I will give you one and a half million dollars for that painting.' Again the man replied, 'I assure you, I am honored that you like it, but I also assure you that it's priceless to me, and will not be sold.'

"An hour later, the meeting ended, and the estate owner

politely walked his guests to the door and said good-bye. As he shut the front door, his wife came to his side. She said, 'How did the meeting go?' 'The business went very well indeed,' he replied, 'and as a matter of fact, I nearly sold our grandchild's kindergarten panting for well over a millions dollars.' "

"Kiss my ass!" *Persistence* said, sitting up in his sleeping bag

"No lie!" I responded.

Worry had been twirling a strand of his hair; his voice seemed halfhearted. "Wait. That's a nice story and all considering we're stuck in the freaking ice, but how the hell does that relate to your McDonald's dream?"

"Oh so easily!" I smiled. "Because right about now, I'd cut off most of my toes for a Big Mac and fries, and not even give it a second thought!" I laughed, but no one else thought I was funny. "Hell, if I could super-size it, I might take off the entire foot!" The other three looked at me oddly, but I knew they understood. I rolled onto my left side. "It just goes to show that a person shouldn't judge value based on some other person's needs and wants!"

There was a brief but heavy lull in conversation as *Change* screwed the lid tight onto the piss bottle. "Any of you philosophers need to piss in this thing?" *Change* asked.

◆◆◆

I was awake. Once again, it was the middle of the night and I was awake. It was apparent to me that I was awake solely out of a pattern I had created. It was a method to warm my body. A way to silence my mind. Being cold, and afraid, and lonely, and wet were routine, normal feelings. I was growing oddly comfortable with my fear and discomfort.

I wormed my way out of the wet sleeping bag and dressed in my wet gear. I crawled out of the cave. There, in the darkness, was a lone headlamp bobbing from left to right. *No, it couldn't be—somebody is dancing in the darkness of night.*

I moved closer. *Everyday* was happily waltzing from side to side. As I got closer to him, I could see he was holding a shovel in his hand as if it was a microphone. He did two full spins and then followed this with a Fred Astaire dip of his dancing partner, the shovel. I laughed. *Everyday* was happy.

"Good evening Mr. Astaire," I said, smiling.

"Fred was the man," he said, as he stroked the shovel like a buxom blonde.

I laughed; I had never seen a bearded, yeti-looking man wooing a shovel. "You really need a woman if you're courting a shovel."

"My dear shovel has been good to me, good to you also."

"Yes, she has!"

He thrust the shovel head into the show. "Bye, my love." He waved at the shovel, then returned his focus to me. "Nice night," he said.

"For a Patagonian storm—yeah, nice night."

"I have a story for you," *Everyday* said.

"Will it teach me more about *Everyday*?" I asked with a grin.

"As a matter of fact, it will explain *Everyday*."

"I'm all ears."

"So, as my grandfather tells it, three men went to the mountains for a walk. Up the mountain they went, and after a while they came across a magical dwarf who was stuck. The three men pulled the dwarf from his problem, and brushed him off. The dwarf was so grateful that he granted each man one wish. The three men thought for a moment. Then the first man said, 'I want to be rich, with the greatest jewels and treasures life has to offer.' Without a second thought, the second man said, 'I want to be famous and desired.' The third man smiled at the dwarf and said, 'Dwarf, my two friends are fools; what I want is the grandest prize of all—I want to know the true meaning of life.'

"The dwarf chuckled, half-smiled, and said, 'All your wishes will be granted.' The three men descended the mountain slope, going back to their lives. Some weeks later, the three men were once again walking in the mountains, and there on a boulder sat the dwarf. The three men had plenty of questions to ask the dwarf, for they felt none of their wishes had been granted. 'Dwarf,' said the first man, 'you lied to us; not one of our wishes has come true.' 'Oh,' said the dwarf. 'Yes,' said the man. 'What is your complaint?' said the dwarf. The first man jumped forward. 'I went back to my life expecting to be rich with valuables.' 'Oh,' said the dwarf. 'Yes,' said the man. 'Tell me,' said the dwarf, 'how many children do you have?' The man's eyes sparkled, pure and wide, as he erupted with pleasure. 'I have two of the most spectacular boys and the absolutely most beautiful little girl this earth has ever seen,' answered the man. 'Oh,' said the dwarf. 'Yes,' said the man. 'And I love them more than anything on the face of this earth.' The dwarf stood and said, 'Your wish has been granted; you have the grandest three treasures life has to offer—your children.' The man's face grew tranquil, peaceful, and happy as he turned and sprinted down the mountain to see his three children.

"The second man stepped forward. 'Dwarf,' he said, 'I have no child, and in fact, my wife can't have children. I wanted to be famous and desired, and I received nothing.' 'Oh,' said the dwarf. 'Yes,' said the man. At that point, the dwarf paused, turning to watch a high-flying hawk. 'So tell me of your wife,' said the dwarf. 'Oh,' gasped the man, 'the love I feel for her—I could work in the most brutal coal mines because at day's end, when I arrive home and enter that door, the look in my wife's eyes tell me I'm loved unconditionally, now and until my death.' 'Oh,' said the dwarf. 'Yes,' said the man. 'Your wish has been granted; you're a star in your wife's eyes and desired by her like the most famous.' The man's eyes glistened and, with no hesitation, he turned, sprinting down the mountain toward his home.

"The dwarf sat back onto his rock. The third man looked down at him. 'Dwarf,' said the third, 'you're in trouble. I have no wife, no kids, and not a thing has changed in my life since I last saw you—I wanted truth, and I've got nothing.' 'Oh,' said the dwarf. 'Yes,' said the man. 'So tell me of your day,' said the dwarf. The man ran his hand through his long, brown hair, then scratched his chin. 'Well, dwarf, my day is average. I rise in the morning, go to work, eat some meals, drink some drink, maybe take a walk in the woods, maybe talk to some friends—pretty simple, dwarf.' 'Simple,' said the dwarf. 'Yes,' said the man. 'You like your day?' asked the dwarf. 'My life is good,' said the man. 'Your wish has been granted,' said the dwarf. 'Your everyday is the true meaning in life,' the dwarf continued. A life well lived, day by day, will create greatness—because seeking a bit of happiness in everyday is the meaning of life."

Everyday stopped. The wind had subsided. The mountains seemed, for a moment, tame. I looked to the sky, and then back to *Everyday*. He grinned at me, then continued by putting a blue ribbon on his tale. "And finally, the third man said, 'Dwarf, you are a smart, smart, little guy. Now that the other two have left us, why don't you and I puff on this marijuana joint I brought with me?' "

"He what!" I said, totally taken aback that the story had switched to smoking drugs.

"No, just joking about smoking the joint, I just wanted to see if you were still with me. But the story—damn good story my grandfather told, yeah!"

"Yes," I said, going back to scanning the distant horizon,

loving the silence of the night. Loving the story I had just heard. "Yep, nearly seems passive out tonight."

"*Today*, I must say, not until recently did I understand why my grandpa nicknamed me *Everyday*. He would say to me, 'Child, you've got the key to life right there; you have the possibility of happiness in *Everyday*!' And he'd pat me on the head, and tell me to seek some happiness everyday."

"You do well," I commented, looking back at the sky.

"That's because I try."

"Look at that. The wind seems to be mellowing," I said.

"Yeah, now it's only blowing at seventy miles an hour!"

"No seriously! Check it out!" I walked to the top of the snow ramp. "The wind is slowing. This thing may be breaking!"

"Keep dreaming; this storm's forever!" *Everyday* said with a playful sigh.

February 21, 2003

I was having a fantastic dream about the south of France, naked women in the south of France, and a large, greasy plate of pasta in the south of France. The sun was warm, the pasta was fulfilling, and the women were soft and smelled like beauty. It was a grand, grand dream. The best dream I had had in nights. I deeply wanted to stay in the south of France, but I heard reality calling my name. And again, I was forced to an awareness that I was still in a cave, in South America, on an ice field, but the south of France was really pleasant. *Whoever is talking is actually yelling, and they're excited.*

Time to say goodbye to the south of France, time for me to wake up!

"The weather's broke! I can see faint stars!!!" The call echoed into the cave like a siren's song. "The weather's broke!!!" I didn't recognize the voice, but who cared? The storm was over!

I rocketed forward in my sleeping bag. "*Yee haw!!!*" I grabbed *Change* and shook him. "Hey! Hey! Wake up! The storm's stopped. It's over!"

Change launched forward in his sleeping bag; his eyes jacked wide open. "The storm's over? The storm's over!!!"

Action leaped out of his sleeping bag, squatted onto his feet, and did a quick little salsa dance. His happy face grooved to an internal Latin beat.

Rapidly, we cooked breakfast, packed our gear, and suited up. The storm had lasted two weeks. We had been buried, barely surviving, in the ice of Patagonia for ten days. On my knees, I crawled out of the snow. It was four o'clock in the morning, still dark.

I stood erect near the entrance of my cave, and quickly the crisp air brought life to my stagnant body. One by one, I stretched my legs. The clouds had given way to a thick haze, and a dull shine of stars could be seen through a mask of clouds. The wind had slowed but was still blowing. We could make out the early stages of an orange sunrise.

"Red sky at night, sailors delight; red sky in the morning, sailors take warning." I'd heard people repeat that saying before, but this morning, as one of my peers pointed out the slight taint of orange in the eastern horizon, it made me nervous. *God help us if there's another storm coming.*

I finished stretching my legs and walked toward a pile of gear. I decided that I would pull one of the pigs. Most of the spare fuel and food supply were gone, making the pigs relatively light at fifty pounds.

Worry was nervous. "Hey! We need to get the hell off the ice! Food and fuel are low!" he said, as he tried to adjust his backpack.

"I know. A little pain on the odd occasion is good for the soul." I spoke with a calm I had never been able to muster on prior interactions with *Worry*.

He looked at me cross-eyed, confused. I had just taken all the power out of *Worry's* blow; I simply refused to let *Worry* blow his hot air into my sails. He grew silent and tied into his rope.

"Hey, *Worry*!" I said.

He looked up, he was thinking.

"Fear is an illusion; physical pain is a reality. Let's avoid mistakes!" I smiled.

"What the hell does that mean!"

"Oh nothing!" *Worry* had always troubled me, living rent-free in my brain, so a little playful payback was good for him.

"What mistakes?" he asked.

"That's my point: Pay attention today!" Again, I smiled, and then I pretended to shoot him with my finger.

"Mistakes?"

I started laughing, "Oh Jesus, lighten up! I'm playing with you!"

"Oh?" He tried to laugh, but failed.

The rope teams were ready. We started hiking back to the north, reversing our original direction. Our pace was hurried. I was willing to hurt. The group moved at a diagonal angle up a slight incline. The high clouds began to clear. Visibility was growing, but the distant horizon still glowed orange.

◆◆◆

Our new route pointed straight to the Key Hole, which was a steep and dangerous rock valley that dropped dramatically to the east away from Patagonia and toward Argentina. Thirty minutes had passed, and my feet rapidly turned over on themselves, constantly repeating their determined stride. Everything was movement. As my legs began to burn with pain, my mind began to chatter.

Shhh! You're not wanted right now!

Faster and faster we moved; there was no time to think. I focused on each breath, each step, and tried to be aware that the more pain I felt, the closer I was to home. I was smashed with a wave of emotion. A tear left my eye and fell to the ice.

I will live to see my mother!

Another hour passed, the hill crested, and we increased the pace on the flat ice. For a moment, I looked over my left shoulder toward the far horizon and was consumed with frustration—clouds were beginning to form. From the west, the wind increased, faster by the moment.

My legs scorched like a four-alarm blaze. As the clouds gathered, more tears began to build in my eyes. Why clouds? Why now? The temperature was dropping. The group stopped. My frustration peaked!

No, don't stop now. Anything but that! Keep moving, no stopping. Just let me move my legs. Once again, I stood alone, and it became painfully and glaringly obvious that Patagonia was brewing one more storm. Another tear left my eye, ran across my cheek, and got trapped in my grungy beard, freezing on my face.

Maybe today we die!

Direction and *Positive* were at the front of our charge. Secured by his rope team, *Positive* scouted our current route another fifty yards. I was unsure why we were delaying. After one minute, he returned from the white. He pointed to the west, then back to the east from the abyss of whiteness. The group began to move back toward the north. I had only one choice, to move when my rope moved. Five minutes passed, and the group gathered on a flat chunk of ice. Visibility was twenty feet. The temperature had dropped twenty degrees in the last hour. The wind gusts were increasing. I walked into the circle. *Positive* and *Direction* stood shoulder to shoulder.

"We're lost," they said.

My heart sank. I was cold. *We're lost*! I bowed my head,

defeated. Once again, Patagonia had won. My heart was broken. Another storm! I couldn't go on.

Our exit, which we thought was the Key Hole, was a one thousand–foot vertical cliff, covered with ice and rock. We did not have the gear needed to get nine men down from a one thousand–foot cliff. We were lost, but even more disturbing, we had been lost for weeks, and we hadn't even known of our peril. We had only one choice: to make more snow caves. We pulled the shovels from our packs and started to dig.

My despair was short-lived. It had to be, because I had no other choice. I could stand, slowly grow cold, and freeze. Or I could dig one more cave, creating, yet again, one more solution to my problem. After my brief moment of agony, anger, and frustration, I flipped my emotions, and mustered the necessary energy to dig another cave.

Scattered like zombies, my peers stood still, comatose in the thick haze of weather. Scattered over a twenty-yard radius, they watched in shock as *Positive*, *Direction*, and I began to dig into the snow.

My cave became deeper and deeper, farther away from the storm. I rounded the roof, smoothed the sides. Pile by pile, I cleared the unwanted snow and dug one more cave. I removed what was not a cave. I created shelter from the storm.

I crawled back into the white. "Who needs a home for the night? I'm open for business!"

February 22, 1996

My eyes opened, still in a cave. My body and mind were rotting. It was one more morning of living underground, starving, freezing, existing like some bizarre creatures from a forgotten episode of the *Twilight Zone.* I slipped my hand out of my wet glove. Its color was pale white, with pinkish blotches and streaks of purple. My skin looked like a piece of old chicken after spending months wedged in the back of the refrigerator.

How close am I to being forgotten? Will I become a newspaper article that some Joe reads as he sips his morning coffee and eats his toast: "American Climbers Die in Patagonia!" Please pass the jam!

Left alone with my rabid mind, I mumbled to myself, "Whore!" Nobody in my cave looked over at me; nobody in my cave cared for me. I was alone with my brain, left to fend for myself. And unfortunately, my brain knew precisely and exactly where I was weak. Slow and painful! I was hemorrhaging thoughts; it became obvious to me that my brain specialized in espionage and it had been a double agent all along. I was wiretapped. Satan was listening, exchanging intimate and vulnerable information with my perception of life. The jig was up; I was about to be exposed!

Talking Head! Shhh! I tried not to listen. I failed.

You will die. You will not survive. You are weak. You are dumb. You are lucky to have survived this far. Life is over.

Jesus Christ! "No more!" I rambled aloud. "No more!" *Stop the beating. I'll be a good boy.*

Anger began to seep slowly from my head like acid, down through my spine, filling every particle of my cold, wet, tired body. *Why me? Why now? I am too damn young to die.* My mind was like a motor speedway; the roar was deafening, and the thoughts screamed by in a blur. Focusing on any one thought became utterly impossible.

I'd had enough of the challenge, enough of proving I was a man. This was not like all those fancy Hollywood films where Joe Stud returns home to Jane Babe and they live happily ever after.

Reality is not a two hundred–foot movie screen.

I was ready to stop the adventuring, put an end to the despair, stop all the fear and return to the comfort of my own home: a couch, a bed, a heater, a microwave, running water, a roof, and my mother. I was done. *Get me home*!

"Maybe we're supposed to die," I said, casually.

"Aren't we happy this morning?" *Slack* answered.

"Hey, fuck-off, you lazy piece of shit!" I shouldn't have said it, but it was too late. It was a mistake.

Everyday quickly sat up on his knees.

"Fuck-off. Oh that's rich!" *Slack* said.

Everyday leaned toward me and interjected: "I got story for you!" He was still resting on his knees.

"No, not another goddamn story, not now!" I griped.

"You'll like it; I promise!" *Everyday* kept talking. "It's about death, and pain, and despair. From where I sit, it's about how you're feeling right now!"

"Great, throw gas on the fire!" I retorted, full of frustration and anger.

"Hey, it's your bad mood, not mine!" *Everyday* said, letting me know he was serious.

"Let's hear it!" *Better than listening to myself think!*

Everyday rolled back on his butt and began his tale. "My father loved to raise plants in his backyard. One spring a pair of mating doves started making their nest in one of his plants. After a couple of days, they'd built themselves a great nest. The female laid two eggs, and then it seemed she never left that nest. As the next week went by, my father was forced to let his plant wilt and then die from lack of water. He was frustrated, but he felt he was sacrificing the life of his plant for the new life of the hatchling doves. Quite a few days into the mother dove's nesting cycle, my father grew worried; he was convinced that she hadn't left her nest in days, plus he hadn't seen the male dove for over a week. My father, who had no biology training, assumed the male had been killed or possibly had abandoned his mate. He was reasonably convinced the female hadn't gone for food or water in multiple days because of her dedication to her future babies. Having a huge heart, my father made a trip to the local hardware store, where he purchased a water bowl, a bird feeder, and bird food. He returned home and placed the water and food one foot away from the dead plant with the nesting mother dove. Then he let her alone. He was trying his damnedest to be helpful.

"The next day, he walked to his backyard window to check on the mother dove. What he saw shocked him. He pounded on the glass as he screamed with panic. In the nest, indulging themselves upon the slaughtered eggs of the dead mother dove, were three carnivorous Steller's jays. My father threw open the back door, still screaming with horror. He ran to the nest. The mother dove's head was split open.

She lay dead in the plant to the side of the nest. Both of the eggs were blown apart, eighty percent eaten. My father was confused. Then he realized that the water and food near the dove's nest had attracted other birds. When the jays discovered the dove's nest, they grew hungry for the eggs and attacked. The mother dove refused to abandon her future chicklings so they killed her. Then they ate her eggs. The father dove, who'd been avoiding the nesting area of his mate, so as not to draw attention to her, attempted to defend his mate against the onslaught of the jays, but to no avail. He was in a nearby tree, bleeding, slowly dying."

"Jesus!" I said. "Why'd you tell me that shit? Is that supposed to make me feel better?"

"No! It's supposed to help you understand reality. Sometimes in life, when you try to help by interrupting the natural process, you just end up killing what you're trying to save or help. People need to experience their pain and their troubles in life. Trying to shelter them from the storm sometimes ends up killing them anyway, slow or fast, but either way they die, and sometimes they even destroy others around them."

Slack had been listening. "I've been sitting right here, at first watching *Today* freak out and then listening to you tell your story," *Slack* said. "I know there's a correlation, because there always is with you! So what the hell is it?"

"We're going to walk out of here. We've had our pain and mental torment. And we're still alive, and when the weather's right, and the winds slow, and the sun returns, we're going to walk out of here, and someday in the distant future, we will tell stories of Patagonia, and those stories of pain and despair and isolation will change lives! We've come to hell, and we're still alive."

◆◆◆

I fiddled with my sleeping bag, then rolled my jacket back into my pillow. Because of all my movement, I had disturbed some snow and scattered it over various parts of my sleeping bag. I sat to my knees and brushed off the snow.

Amazing! My sleeping bag is soaking wet, but I still feel the need to maintain it and attempt to keep it dry. This is crazy.

A momentary silence crept back, but I was not in the mood for thinking.

"I got a question for you," I said. "What's your favorite of the seven deadly sins?"

"The last time I checked, the seven deadly sins were bad, not good," *Persistence* answered, sarcastically.

"What? Who you fooling!" I retorted. "What about lust?" We had nothing else to do, so we might as well lighten the mood.

"Yeah, lust is nice!" *Everyday* said with a glimmer of desire.

"Yeah, lust was nice. Throw some gluttony and sloth in there and you know what that equals?" I said.

"Tell me," *Persistence* said.

I happily rubbed my hands together. "A good night at home on the couch, right after a huge meal your girlfriend just cooked, all followed and mixed with great sex!"

"What I wouldn't give for a dry couch and some warm food on a plate," *Everyday* said.

"What about the sex?" *Persistence* asked.

"My dick's so pruned, I'm not sure it will ever plum again," *Everyday* exclaimed.

We all chuckled because we all understood.

Persistence stopped laughing and his face became serious. "Who wants to talk about the seven deadly sins?"

Persistence said. "That means I'd have to think about where I've gone wrong in my life, and to sit here thinking about dying and death and unresolved arguments that I may be forced to die with—that sucks!"

"He's got a point. We're two days from running out of food, then what?" *Everyday* suddenly seemed serious.

"That's what I mean. I have loved lust my entire life." From my pocket, I pulled out a soggy, wet piece of paper with a list of names on it. "Food or no food, we need to get the hell out of here!" I shook my list.

Everyday focused on the list. "What the hell's that?"

"My list. I owe these women an apology."

"You what!" exclaimed *Persistence*.

"You wrote a list!" *Everyday* said.

"Yes!" They looked at me curiously. "Nobody thinks they're going to die, or even worse, nobody thinks they're going to die young. Fuck! We're young! And look at us! We're stuck under the ice, totally goddamn lost somewhere in South America on the goddamn fourth largest ice field in the world." I shook my list vigorously. "Christ, we're forty-eight hours from eating our last meal. And still, we think there's no way we could die!"

"Speak for yourself! I see death everyday!" *Persistence* said, his voice laced with desperation.

"I see death everyday too!" I retorted. "But life gets simple in a snow cave. Looking back at my life and reviewing where I've gone wrong with other people lets me see what I need to change in how I interact with the world. Every time I've caused another person hurt or anger, that's a direct result of a flaw in me." Briefly, I looked at both *Everyday* and *Persistence*. "A flaw that is changeable!" They looked at each other.

"You actually think you'll change if we live?" *Persistence* asked.

"Honestly, I'm not sure if I care. I just want one shot to make my wrongs right. Just one shot!"

"Why's that?" *Everyday* asked.

"Because I think that in the process of making my wrongs right, I'd change, even if all of me doesn't want to change!"

Persistence was deep in thought, his face tense. "I'd like to talk with my father."

"*Change* will happen. I just need to show up and make my wrongs right."

"How?" *Everyday* asked.

"I'm just going to show up; I'll know when I'm there in front of them!" My goal suddenly became even clearer to me. "I don't want to die with this shit unresolved!" I held my list like it was the Holy Grail. "I've been pondering the consequences of dying for two weeks."

"How will you know when you're there?" *Everyday* asked.

"I'll focus only on my shit; it will have nothing to do with the other people. I'll just focus on my wrongs and my garbage. Basically, clean my dirt off the problem—pretty simple!"

Some time passed. It could've been moments or minutes; again, time's an odd thing in a snow cave. And then all at once, *Everyday's* face lightened up so much it was obvious even in the dank hue of the cave. "Hey, which one of the seven deadly sins would cover sex, drugs, and rock-and-roll?" *Everyday* smiled.

"I'd say that's a crazy combination of all seven," *Persistence* answered.

Everyday was still smiling. "Yeah, I've always been thorough!"

◆◆◆

Slack raked both his hands through his long, grungy hair. From behind a dirty curtain of hair, his eyes swelled with tears. He had been mentally pacing for the last hour. It was obvious *Slack* was struggling. His lips shook. "Why don't we just get the hell out of here!"

Persistence casually answered, "Which direction?"

"Who cares!" *Slack* said, as he scratched at his scalp. "Just start hiking, get our butts moving, stop sitting!"

Persistence raised his awareness and said, "How can you say who cares—are you nuts? We need a direction, a route of some sort."

"So we go east; Christ, eventually, if nothing else, we'll hit Buenos Aries in Argentina!" *Slack* was mentally panicking. "Yeah! We go east!"

"What a great idea!" *Persistence* answered, his voice laced with sarcasm. "Christ! If I kept digging in the ice, eventually I'll hit China, but you don't see me digging for Chinese take-out, do ya!"

"So what—we just sit here and freeze to death? Screw that, I'd rather hike, die trying, be a man about it!"

"You're freaking!"

"And you're slowly dying!"

I sat up. They needed a middleman, and at that moment, it was my turn to connect the dots. One of the most intriguing aspects about life is that all people are not in poor moods all at the same time, on the same day. "Why create a third problem when right now we only have two problems," I said. "We need to wait. The storm will end; storms always do."

"The storm will end and we'll be dead!" *Slack* was obviously convinced that waiting the storm out meant certain death.

Persistence turned his attention toward me. "What do you mean by a third problem?"

"At this point, we only have two problems to deal with," I answered, hoping to coax *Slack* into the conversation. "One of the problems is the storm, and the second's a snow cave."

"What the hell else could be wrong!" *Slack's* angst was turning to anger.

I took a breath, then another long and deep breath, filling my lungs before I spoke. "Well, if we take your approach and go wander around, lost, in a blizzard that's fit to kill a polar bear, then we'd have a third issue: Some of us will freeze to death—die trying, as you say—and then the others will get nasty hypothermia. And after all that, we'll be right back where we started, in another snow cave, still stuck, but some of us will be dead and the survivors will be nearly dead, back in a cave, just like this one, but worse off!" I exhaled.

Slack watched my lips, his eyes transfixed. He had pulled the parking brake on his mind.

I continued. "We need to solve one issue at a time. If not, we just create other problems that we'll be forced to deal with before returning to the original problem."

"So we just wait?" *Slack* asked.

"There's nothing but more problems to come if we wander aimlessly in a storm this size!" I said.

"But what about waiting too long?" he asked, wanting to be reassured.

"Right at this moment, as funny as it sounds, we're okay. We still have some food, we still have ten days' worth of fuel to melt snow for water, and most important, we've got shelter from the storm. We need to have patience and persistence; the storm may stop in five minutes. And when the storm stops, and the time's right, then we can die trying!"

February 23, 1996

I was awake as the snow cave roof began to glow a faint blue. I had survived one more night in a Patagonian snow cave. Somewhere, very, very far away, the sun was warm and hot, boiling and bubbling. Through millions of miles of space, across hundreds of miles of the earth's atmosphere, behind the thick, dank veil of clouds and a survival layer of ice, the slightest, puniest, most dismal trace of sunshine let me know it was morning.

My body was deep into the decomposing process. It hadn't seen direct sun in over a month. My skin had been saturated with moisture for more than two weeks. My wet clothes had suffocated my skin. The clothing that kept me warm enough to barely survive also insured I was soggy twenty-four hours a day. My fingers were a ghostly white splattered with blue splotches. The skin on my face was beginning to peel off in large chunks. Fortunately, I couldn't see my own rotting face, but I could see *Worry's*, and he was growing more disgusting each day. Every time *Worry* turned his head, a large portion of his face flapped. And as if that weren't enough, he had a pasty, white substance coagulating under his nose. It streamed toward his mouth.

I sat up. "I couldn't sleep last night," I said. "Too cold. All night, I kept doing sit-ups in my sleeping bag to generate heat, but every time I fell asleep, I'd shiver myself awake in ten minutes."

"I heard you," responded *Persistence*. "I did a few sit-ups myself!"

"Things aren't getting any better; we've got maybe four more meals," *Worry* said.

Persistence and I looked at *Worry*. His eyes were still closed. His energy was depleted. We had been rationing food for the past eight days. We lacked nutrients.

"My body's shutting down. It's dying," I said, somewhat casually since death was now out of my control. "Tonight we need to join sleeping bags. I can't generate enough warmth on my own."

"Okay!" *Persistence* said, as he turned his head toward me and half-smiled. "Always thought you were cute!" He laughed to himself.

I didn't think he was funny, but my frustration was tempered by lack of energy. Control was no longer mine because my body shook and shivered in random intervals.

Frustration takes energy, and I can't spare the energy to be *frustrated over something I cannot change.*

"We've got maybe four meals," *Worry* said again, his eyes still closed. He was talking to absolutely no one, but I heard him. "Four more meals!"

February 24, 1996

I licked the bottom of my bowl. I licked my fingers. I licked my lips. I had just eaten my last meal. I was now the equivalent of a Death Row inmate. I looked around, hoping a vending machine would magically appear in the far corner of the cave. I was hungry, tired, and lonely, and if I'd had the energy, I would have been angry.

"That's it. Food's gone," *Worry* said. "That was our last meal."

"Don't remind me," *Persistence* answered.

"No more food!" *Worry* said again.

"Hey, I got it. We draw straws; whoever gets the short straw, we eat," *Persistence* spoke with an eerie calm.

"You're not funny," *Worry* said.

"For once, I agree with him," I said. "You're not funny."

"Well, hell, someone needs to get eaten," he continued. "People do this crap all the time when they're lost and out of food—eating one another. What's the big deal?"

"Enough!" *Worry* said angrily.

Persistence ignored him. "Yeah. Remember that book, slash movie, slash actual event, Alive, when those rugby players ate one another? Hell, that was just to the north of here—same mountains, the Andes."

"That was in northern Chile; we're in southern," *Worry* began to argue.

"Same difference."

"No! I believe it's entirely different."

I was semi-entertained. Aside from the fact that we were starving to death, in the Andes, stuck in a snow cave, *Persistence* was slightly funny. An argument proceeded to erupt. I took a nap. I was hungry, far too hungry to argue.

The day vanished. We had no food to cook, so there was absolutely nothing to do.

February 26, 1996

My eyes opened. The cave glowed bright blue. I rubbed my face.

Holy shit! The cave's bright blue! Sunshine?

I tore myself from my sleeping bag. I didn't change or put on boots. I launched myself like a rocket out of the cave. Sunrise in Patagonia! It was clear and beautiful. *God bless the sun!* My face erupted with a massive smile. "Yes! I will live!" I yelled, arms reaching toward the endless blue sky.

I stood, amazed and shocked. I was in the middle of two rock- and ice-covered mountain peaks. Like teeth, like wolves, they attacked the sky. Sharp, aggressive, and dangerous at their summits, they were jagged throughout, like a giant logger saw. Their ridges were backed by a deep blue sky. The space between the two peaks, where I stood, was a quarter mile of white fluffy snow.

"Thank God," I whispered to myself. "The sun!" I screamed, jumping into the air. "The sun's out!" I knew I looked ridiculous, but I didn't care. "Wake up! The sun's out! Get up! The sky's clear!"

Person by person, *Everyday*, *Direction*, *Positive*, *Worry*, *Change*, *Action*, *Persistence*, and *Slack* crawled from their caves.

"Thank you, God!" *Persistence* raised his arms to the sky, adding a silent thank-you.

"Wow! Who would've guessed about the beauty!" *Change* gave me a nod and a smile.

Positive's body pulsed with physical energy. "Crank it up, baby; it's time to fly! That's astounding!"

"That's a huge, beautiful chunk of rock right there!" *Worry* scanned the horizon for storm clouds; there wasn't a drop of mist in the sky for miles. "Let's get outta here."

Slack frantically adjusted his pants. "Beautiful day for a long, long hike."

Everyday was dancing. He was ready for the day, ready for life. "This is what *Everyday's* all about. Beauty, on top of beauty, covered by even more beauty. This is why I live. Right now, right here!" Uncontrollably, he started to shuffle his feet, giddy as a schoolboy. Then, randomly, he made history by performing the first-ever cartwheel on the Northern Patagonian Ice Field. "Yee haw!"

"¡Qué bonito! Yo soy feliz. ¡Qué bonito!" *Action* beamed.

"Hey, *Positive*, what he'd say?" I asked.

"Something along the lines of 'Amazing Grace,' just faster."

All at once, we turned toward *Direction*. He stood, strong and tall, ready to lead. "Gentlemen, great day for a walk in the mountains!" *Direction* smiled confidently. "Time to pack and get moving!"

In unison, we yipped and hollered, yodeled and sang.

◆◆◆

Direction pointed to his left, to a ridgeline that looked to be ten or fifteen miles away as the crow flies. "That's where we're heading. That's our valley on the other side of that ridge!" He tightened his strap. "Let's roll!"

I suited up: backpack, rope, gloves, and ice axe. I checked

all my gear, all my various ropes and knots and buckles, and then performed all the appropriate safety checks. I was ready to walk out of Patagonia alive.

I looked around. At first, I saw the obvious—glorious mountain peaks. I had been forced into a cave. I had been forced blind for weeks. During the entire storm, during the chaos, and through the hell that I experienced, these mountains were standing there tall and beautiful. Not a thing about them had changed, except now I could see them. The mountains were always there; I was just living beneath the clouds.

I looked back to my left; my eyes squinted in the early morning sun. Sixteen intense eyes focused on me. It was time. As a group, we had crawled up and out of the snow, and now it was time to walk ourselves back to life, back to our homes, and back to living like humans.

"Time to move forward," I said.

◆◆◆

As we hiked on and on, my thoughts wandered. When you're driving from Los Angeles, California, to Las Vegas, Nevada, there's a portion of Interstate 15 that leaves the small desert town of Baker and proceeds to gradually, steadily, and painfully climb from the valley floor to the summit at five thousand feet in elevation. The freeway is forty repetitive miles of straight asphalt, and the distance can be deceiving. Cars overheated constantly. During my sophomore year in college, my roommate and I blew up our car's motor while driving that long stretch of deceptive road. After we had a brief emergency conference on the side of the highway, we retreated down the steep grade on the shoulder of Interstate 15. It was three o'clock in the morning, and I rode the trunk waving a flashlight as Eric steered the car backward. After a fifteen-mile trunk ride by the light of the moon, the car never moved again. Distance can be deceiving.

Now, as we hiked, we were spread over four hundred yards of fresh snow. It was nearing midday. We had been drudging up the hill for more than five hours. The hill was long, straight, and deceptive. I was leading, breaking trail through the fresh snow. As I walked, I created footprints for my peers to follow, like a staircase. The tempo was a crawl.

Dammit! Another step. *Bastard!* Another step. *Dammit!* Another step. *Bastard!* Another step. I chanted to myself, "Oh where, oh where, has my hilltop gone, oh where, oh where can it be?"

For hours I repeated this, forced to deal with each step. And for hours I felt like I should be able to touch the goal. Sometimes it's more difficult to see and comprehend your destination when it's very, very far in the distance or in the future. Some days moving forward one step at a time can be more tolerable than looking up toward the top of the ridge.

Action and *Slack* were the other two on my rope team. Every time my legs complained about exhaustion, I looked behind me at *Action*, who was pulling one of the pigs. He was awe-inspiring.

The sky was an ardent blue. The sun was intense and extremely hot. I unzipped my shirt, looking down at the sweat on my chest and stomach as the sun's rays reflected off my torso. I was carved with sinewy muscle like a ancient Roman statue; all extra skin and fat had been eaten by my own body over the last six weeks.

I slowed my pace just enough to take a long look over my shoulder. *Everyday* was the last man, at least half a mile behind me—a dark speck on the white snow. We were a group of men trudging up a ridgeline to a common goal, and because of that, our bond was strong.

Two o'clock in the afternoon, and the hill finally began to crest.

Hallelujah! From here, it's all downhill!

I increased the pace. The hill rolled into flat ground, and the pure, clear afternoon air allowed me to gaze over a hundred miles to the east toward Argentina. I walked another hundred yards and stopped. *I'll wait here for the rest of the team.* I removed my pack and sat on it. *Action* and *Slack* fell to their butts behind me. Seven hours of hiking up a steady ridge would make most people fall to their butts!

While I waited, I drank some water and ate a nut that I'd found in my jacket pocket. I wasn't sure it was from this journey or if it was two years old, but either way, it tasted good. I was happy to have one nut.

The rest of the team arrived. *Direction* and *Positive* were leading their rope teams and approached to my right. I smiled at *Positive. All downhill from here!* He did not smile back at me.

Positive pointed to a lake off in the distance. It was a massive lake and seemed to be seventy to a hundred miles away. *Direction* then pointed to the south, which was back the way we'd just hiked.

"What?" I asked.

Direction adjusted his glasses and stroked his grimy hair. "We're thirty miles to the north in the wrong direction." He was calm about it, nearly methodical.

"We're what!" I was unsure whether to feel anger or despair.

Positive pointed to the lake. "I know that lake very well, and we need to go south. We've been lost for the last five weeks and we didn't even know it. We're thirty miles to the north in the wrong direction."

"We've got to go back down this ridge and across the northwest corner of the ice field," *Direction* said while pointing south.

I froze. "Oh Jesus!" My body felt heavy. My brain felt hopeless.

I was at a turning point. I had a choice. I could be frustrated, depressed, and beaten. Or I could look at the positives. For the first time in weeks, we weren't lost; we knew exactly and precisely where we needed to go. There was not a single, solitary cloud in the sky, and I had two legs to walk me out of Patagonia.

It is only a setback if you don't have a solution!

It was three o'clock in the afternoon. We'd been hiking since seven o'clock in the morning. From where we stood, we had thirty miles to cover before we were off the ice. Moving fast, keeping a steady pace at three miles an hour, we could be on soil by one o'clock in the morning.

Direction looked at the rest of the team. "Someone needs to tell them," he said.

"Let me," I volunteered.

Direction nodded his approval.

I turned to the others. "Good news and bad news!" I tried to speak with enthusiasm. "Good news: We're no longer lost. That lake off in the distance is Vemir, so for the first time in weeks, we've got a landmark to judge our position. Bad news: We're thirty miles too far to the north." My attempt at enthusiasm failed. Simultaneously, five heads dropped in defeat, all but *Everyday's*.

Everyday stood from his pack. "That's it? Thirty miles and I can sleep on dirt. Yee haw!" He jumped into the air. And if he was only acting like he was happy, he deserved an Oscar.

Astounded, I looked at *Direction* and *Positive*. Their eyes perked up.

"Time to go home, boys! Tonight we sleep on soil! Yee haw!" *Everyday* threw his left foot directly behind him, and started to bounce in place, swinging his arms in rhythm to his bounce. My butt started to twitch with energy.

The damn hippie is dancing. God bless him!

The others raised their chins, and instantly I could see it on their faces; at first, they were annoyed and filled with disdain for *Everyday*, but his spirit was contagious. *Everyday's* rhythm was spreading.

The power of a fresh and positive Everyday is rejuvenating.

Slack, *Action*, *Worry*, *Persistence*, and *Change* all lifted themselves from their butts; life flickered back into their eyes.

"Everyone take five more minutes. Then we head back toward the south!" *Direction* said while digging through his backpack.

I looked south. My face baked in the sun. The day was young. I refocused. After everything I had been through in the last six weeks, I could manage anything for twenty-four hours. I adjusted myself, shifting my mind while wiping the snot from my dripping nose. "It's only a setback if you don't have a solution." Nobody heard me, but that wasn't my point.

◆◆◆

The sun was blistering hot. From every part of the ice, the sun's rays reflected back toward my face and body, slowly, but constantly seeping away at my dwindling energy supply. The group was spread out over a half-mile on the ice. *Direction* had been in the lead since we oriented our position and began moving to the south. The day was growing old, and the sun had begun its slow crawl toward the horizon. The air was thick with fatigue. My ability to be upbeat had been whittled away. My body had moved past aching; I felt dull.

Deep into exhaustion, I began to talk to myself. "When tired, follow *Direction*. Out there, somewhere, is *Direction*. When tired, follow *Direction*."

Behind me was *Slack*, and he had been hiking hard, pushing the pace. "What?" *Slack* yelled at me, unaware that I was tired and semidelusional.

"I'm beat. Damn tired. *Today* can just follow *Direction*," I stumbled, took two wobbly steps, and nearly fell face-first into the ice. I looked back at *Slack*.

"Really great," *Slack* yelled, his voice riddled with sarcasm. "I'm roped to your ass, so all *Slack* can do is follow *Today*." His step looked crisp. "Lead on!" he yelled.

My head fell forward. "Walking."

◆◆◆

The three rope teams moved forward. My steps, my visuals, my team, my thoughts, and most of all, my desperate desire to get off the ice were painfully moving me forward. My feet repeatedly leapfrogged one another. Mundane, boring, painful, and then, mundane, boring, and painful again! *Wash, rinse, repeat.* For hours I duplicated this process, minutes at a time, hours at a time. The sun began to sink toward the ice.

The topographical maps we carried as guides to the region had huge blank areas, because years ago, when the maps were created, the satellites could not pierce the thick cloud cover of Patagonia. Repeatedly, over the course of a year, Patagonia was far too covered in clouds for them to accurately map the entire area's geography. When I first learned this months earlier, it struck me as odd, but after my experience on the ice, I understood. So for much of the afternoon, we walked past mountains that weren't on our map.

My rope team had gradually closed the distance on the group hiking in front of us: the team of *Positive*, *Worry*, and *Everyday*. *Everyday* was last on his team and I was first on mine. This allowed us the freedom to walk and talk together, and kill some of the dreary time.

"Can't wait for the sun to go down," *Everyday* said. "Damn thing's hot!"

"Grass is always greener. Even in Patagonia," I responded.

"Besides the two hundred mile an hour winds, massive blizzards, and the scorching sun, Patagonia ain't that bad a place."

"Grass is always greener."

◆◆◆

The colors of the sunset were amazing. But I didn't even look twice; my energy had vanished. *Beauty is for those people with time and energy!* My feet clipped along. I wanted the pain to stop. I needed to rest, but my delusions had returned; the voices in my head started to chatter.

"How long we been walking?" the voice asked.

Hallucinations?

More voices. "Can't go on, no more walking, make it stop."

"Who's that?" I said out loud.

I stopped walking. Looked to the sky. Couldn't see God, not yet. *Slack* walked straight into my back. I flopped forward, barely keeping my balance. He had been directly behind me, head down, mumbling words at the ice.

"What the hell you doing?" I screamed. "You can't be here, this close; we're on the same goddamn rope team! This is dangerous!"

"HUH?" *Slack* looked at me, empty eyes, lost in the delusion of his pain. His ability to think clearly had taken much punishment.

"Oh shit!" I looked back to the front, no one else to help.

"I can't go on. No more. Make it stop," he pleaded.

"No! No! No! You're goddamn crazy! Stay here! We need rope between us. This is goddamn dangerous!" I walked rapidly forward, but *Slack* also began to walk. I stopped.

"Hey!" Empty eyes looked back at me. "Hey! What the hell you doing?"

"No more." *Slack* attempted to sit down, but fell to his left, his cheek slammed into the ice. "Eh wink mo mum," he mumbled, face pressed to the ice.

"Good." I looked around, squinting in the sun. "You just rest there, let me walk this rope out."

I adjusted my pack, tightened the straps, and moved on. After thirty feet, I stopped and turned around to face *Slack*. The rope was once again tight, back at a safe distance.

"Okay, get up, time to walk, let's move." No response. "*Slack*! Get up!"

He's not moving. Christ, he actually looks dead!

"*Slack*?"

Action had been watching this entire exchange from the back of our rope team.

"He tired!" *Action* said.

Action had just made the world's most obvious observation.

"He seems goddamn dead is what he seems," I screamed.

Without thinking of the consequences, I walked toward *Slack*. I was tired. I was hungry. I was angry. I was making a mistake.

"Are you fucking dead?" I yelled.

"No! Dangerous! Stop!" *Action* called to me in his thick Spanish accent.

He was right. But I was tired and *Slack* looked dead.

"Plan bad! Wait for peoples!" *Action* made one last attempt at logic, and even in broken English, it should have made sense to me.

"Haven't seen a crevasse in days," I responded, pompous, not taking into consideration that I had been in a snow cave for weeks and all the fresh snow had covered even the largest and most dangerous crevasses. I reached *Slack* in moments.

"Get up! You begged to walk out of here alive. Now walk out of here alive!" I reached down. He wasn't moving.

"Hey!" I grabbed a handful of snow and ice and rubbed it into his face.

His arms flailed to his head as his legs jolted. I grab his shoulders and shook, once, twice, three times.

"Get up and move your ass!" I was out of control. My ability to be helpful had vanished with my energy.

He rolled to his knees. I leaned over, grabbed his wet hands, and began to pull hard. Slowly, he began to stand. It was as if I were raising the dead. After a few unsure moments, *Slack* seemed to steady himself. "Let's move," I said, letting go of his hands.

His eyes faded. His chin dropped. And I watched as he briefly wobbled, then fell straight backward, deadweight, in slow motion.

BOOM! Crevasse! An explosion of weak snow. Instantly, the ground splintered into oblivion. Crevasse! Through the ice we were sucked, tumbling through open air. *Whoosh!* Free fall!

"NO!!!"

Then as abruptly as it began, everything stopped. My heart raced. It was dark. My body was stuck. Tight. I felt pressure all over, millions of years of packed ice. I was wedged between ice and ice, somewhere in the belly of the Northern Patagonian Ice Field. Which way was up, which way was down? I attempted to get oriented. I was definitely stuck. The two ice walls were twenty-four inches across.

Oh shit! Looking down, I saw that my left leg had been forced up and into my body. *Legs shouldn't do that.* It was pressed hard against my stomach, jammed sideways between my gut and the ice wall. It was contorted.

No! It must be broken. I must be in shock.

My arms were above my head, pointing toward the top of the crevasse, ice axe still in hand. Faint traces of the sky above illuminated the crevasse. I looked down and couldn't see the bottom, but knew it was down below me somewhere. It was eerie, like swimming in a dark lake at midnight.

"Damn it!" But still no pain. Hmm. *I guess sometimes shock is beneficial.*

"Patagonia sucks," *Slack* mumbled.

Momentarily, I had forgotten about *Slack*. "*Slack*?" I said.

"What?" he answered.

Stuck below me was *Slack*. He was jammed upside down, head pointing toward the bottom of the crevasse. As he moved, the foot in my stomach also moved. And then it became clear.

"That's a relief. This foot in my stomach is yours, not mine," I said.

"A relief? How's that make it better?" *Slack* asked.

My eyes had adjusted to the dark. I looked down at *Slack*. His long, unwashed hair hung free.

I am stuck in a rut with Slack. How do I get out?

"What happened?" *Slack* asked.

"What happened!" I squawked, shocked he didn't recall his stupidity, or for that matter, my stupidity. "Odd question, don't you think? Here we are stuck in Patagonia, and really, truly, it doesn't matter how we got here. Maybe later, during a nap, or a siesta, it may matter how. But for now we just need a solution. We don't need a bunch of whys. We just need up and out of the crevasse! We need a solution; not reasons why. Here we are, period. Later, after we have crawled or climbed—hell, maybe even been pulled or been dragged out of here. At that point, why is maybe something to ask. Right now, I need a solution to get me out of this rut!"

A shadow crossed over the top of the crevasse. On the surface, I could see a silhouette, and then another. I focused.

"You alive?" *Persistence* yelled down to me.

"Alive!" I yelled back.

"Anyone injured?"

"Nope! Not that we can tell."

"¿Qué pasa mi amigo?"

"*Action*, you great Latin lover! Get me the hell outta here!"

"¡Sí señor!" *Action* chuckled to himself.

Stuck in a rut with Slack, but Action and Persistence can help me out.

I rearranged my position, removing all my gear from my back. Then I got *Slack* out from under my butt. I found I was much more comfortable without *Slack* hanging under my ass. From the top, *Action* lowered a separate rope into the crevasse, and *Slack* hooked into that rope. Once *Slack* was on a separate rope, without too much effort, I was able to climb the safety rope I'd been dangling from, leaving *Slack* below in the crevasse.

"Can't we leave *Slack* down there?" I asked, as I crawled over the top lip of the crevasse.

"I know *Slack* can be a tough companion," *Persistence* said.

"Oh, I was joking!" I said. "*Slack's* actually useful—let's me know when I need to take action!" I winked at *Action*.

I stood, looking around. The entire group had spread out over a fifty-yard radius in a semicircle, with various rope anchors secured.

"When *Today* and *Slack* get stuck together in the cold and dark, one can't be too careful in bringing them back to the sunlight," *Direction* yelled to me from fifty yards away.

"Hey!" *Slack's* cry reverberated from the crevasse.

Secured by my taut safety rope, I leaned over the edge of the crevasse and looked down into the ice gash.

"Get me outta here!"

"You're clear; climb away."

◆◆◆

Dusk had turned into night. Off in the distance, I could see where the mountains collided with the ice field. And still we hiked. Call it luck, or fate, or possibly destiny, but a bright rising moon was crawling along the eastern skyline—the first we'd seen it in many weeks. The sun was gone, but the moon was the perfect nightlight. Hollywood couldn't have created a better, more exquisite scene, and if I could have let go of my pain for only an instant, I would have been able to better appreciate the immeasurable beauty.

I had been out of the crevasse for no more than one hour, and already my legs were ungrateful for their freedom. We had been on ice for over a month: living, sleeping, moving, interacting, eating, and holding onto survival for one-twelfth of a year.

◆◆◆

The moon dangled like fruit from a tree, half high in the slow night sky. The white beast flickered millions of reflections upon the ice particles. The world was glistening, etched in moonlight. Everything was covered by a slow, peaceful hue of white. For the first time that day, I could see our destination, but the distance was hard to judge. Frankly, I was unsure if it was one mile or fifteen miles.

Thank God for *Direction*—at that point, I had put nearly all my faith into his lead.

Our three rope teams were spread over half a mile. It was ten o'clock at night and we had been at a deep, steady trudge for the better part of three hours. In the glow of white, one hundred yards in front of me, three figures stood in the moon shadows of the Patagonian mountains. The lead rope team had stopped. I had not been face-to-face with them for hours. I hadn't talked to anyone for hours. I was lonely.

I approached to the left of *Persistence*, followed by *Change*, and finally *Direction*, who had been leading. He was focused far off in the distance. We were close; *Direction's* eyes told me that. I stopped and unloaded my pack.

To my right, *Change* was squatting over the ice, bare ass exposed, shitting right in front of his peers. As the shit fell from his ass, plopping to the ice, a slight steam crept into the night air. His face was anguished. Dead flesh hung from his nose and cheeks; exhaustion oozed from his pores. His hair was matted to his scalp. His lips were pasty white, dry, and peeling. *Yeah, right! Mountaineering is exotic and romantic.*

I looked away; life can be ugly at times. I focused on *Direction*, following his gaze to what I believed would be our final destination that night. The third rope team approached—*Positive*, *Slack*, and *Everyday*. I swiveled back. *Change* stood above his shit, pulling his pants to his waist.

As *Everyday* walked up, he couldn't help his words: "Dude, you just shit!"

Prior to Patagonia's wrath, *Change*, who once was his own self-proclaimed action hero, would have retorted, rebutted, snickered, or just plain been a dick to *Everyday*. But at that moment, *Change's* metamorphosis was complete.

"How are you still standing?" *Change* asked *Everyday.*

Change had been forced into a cocoon of ice, and when given the chance, he crawled out. He was a good human, a good friend.

He looked at *Direction.* "What should I do with my shit?" he asked.

Change had just *hit the nail on the head.* I was leaving my shit behind. I was moving forward, allowing part of *Today* to be killed, forgotten, and frozen forever on the Northern Patagonian Ice Field. In that steaming pile of shit, I saw life progressing, evolving, moving forward, and permanently changing.

"Leave your shit!"

"Just there!" *Direction* pointed to the northwest. "We will find rock, and soil, and warm ground—just there. One, two hours tops." He turned, making eye contact with the rest of us.

For a brief moment, we forgot our pain, and we were proud. For the first time in more than a month, we could smell the dirt. Streaks of time had permanently painted and altered our faces. I was changed. My life had evolved one more step. Everyone adjusted his gear, and with one last look around, my peers subconsciously left their own piles of steaming shit in Patagonia.

I smirked. *Evolution is an ugly pile of shit, rich with nutrients for growth.*

◆◆◆

It was one o'clock in the morning; another three hours had passed. We were eighteen hours into our hiking day. All nine of us had not eaten any food in over two days. My mind began to eat upon its own sense of self-doubt, the worst kind of cannibalism.

"One hundred yards as the crow flies to dirt!" *Direction's* voice echoed back to the group.

As the crow flies? I would kill to be the crow!

There was one problem: one hundred yards of deep, vicious crevasse scars in the ice. At least twenty of them, back to back, and they crisscrossed our path. Some were two feet across, and others were fifty feet wide. The group was bunched close, maybe too close. One collapsing ice bridge or a shift in one of the larger crevasses with the team this close would create a fatal disaster. Only one hundred and fifty yards separated *Direction*, who was still leading the final push, from *Everyday*, who was the last man standing on the third rope team. I looked down at my legs. They were numb. Time to focus because death comes easier when you are tired.

The first crevasse to block our path was ten feet wide. We walked two hundred yards to the north to where it ended. I reminded myself that the soil and dirt I desired was only one hundred yards to the west. We looped around the end of the crevasses, returning to the south. My head grew dizzy.

Damn crevasses!

The team headed south. Plugging and trudging along, I moved my legs, even though I could no longer feel them. We walked two hundred yards to the far end of the crevasse, where it abruptly ended. I stopped. My head floated. Something was wrong.

"Hey, you okay?" *Worry* yelled from behind.

I turned to look at him. Everything went black.

◆◆◆

I gazed into the night sky, my back pressed firmly to the ice; piercing blotters of light sparkled bright. I was done. I could move no more. My chest would rise and then fall back toward the earth. As it fell, my breath climbed toward the heavens. My nose was cold. I was hungry. I was too tired to be afraid any longer. Delusion was my master! Everything began to slow. My eyes closed.

Ultimately, death brings a clear honesty to the table. Many negatives can be associated with dying, but death's one redeeming quality remains its innate ability to force a person to see life through honest eyes. All inadequate desires vanish.

February 27, 1996

My eyes opened. Sunshine! Life! Survival! I looked left, and then back to the right. I was alive. Nine men lay, one after another, in the open air and sunshine of the eastern side of the Northern Patagonian Ice Field. We were lying among rocks, and soil, and weeds, and insects, and moss. Life was abundant. I reached back to my butt to where a rock was poking into me. I pulled it out. It was beautiful, lightly covered with soil. I had not seen a rock for over a month.

Direction was lying at the far end of the group on the outside of his bag, looking into the clear morning sky. He looked over toward me and winked. We had just completed the third crossing of the Northern Patagonian Ice Field.

"How'd I get here?" I asked, rolling to my knees.

"If I told you, you wouldn't believe it."

"I don't remember a damn thing after all those crevasses! What, did I magically turn into a crow?" I joked. "Did I fly here?"

"Oh no, *Today*, you didn't turn into a crow or anything else that could move. You collapsed; we thought you'd died, because really, you looked dead!"

I felt my face wrinkle with doubt. "What happened?"

"*Change* carried you!" *Direction* could see the shock in my eyes, and for a moment, he let me process my thoughts.

After all my doubting of *Change*, he had carried me forward when I could not help myself. When my own personal strength vanished, *Change* lifted me over the final chasm.

"Let's wake the others," *Direction* said.

◆◆◆

The group had been awake and shuffling around at the base of the glacier for fifteen minutes. We were scattered over a medium-sized outcropping of rocks at the top of the valley. I was leaning against a flat rock, examining my feet. They no longer looked like feet. And then I heard it: a buzz, a motor. As it grew louder, I got oriented to its position. I stood. A small biplane was flying up the valley. I grabbed my jacket, jumped up on a rock ledge, and began swinging my jacket over my head.

I have seen this in the movies. Let's hope it works.

I looked around; all my peers had seen the same movie. We stood, hooting, hollering, and yelling, while we aggressively swung our jackets like helicopter blades over our heads. The plane grew closer and rolled its wings from side to side. We had been found.

God bless!

I saw *Direction* pull a radio from his pack, and in moments, he began to talk into the microphone. I couldn't hear, so I walked to *Direction's* side. He was in mid-conversation. "Yeah, we're pretty beat up, but at this point, nothing fatal."

Through the speaker, a man's voice crackled. "Good to hear. As far as dropping food supplies, won't work. I'd have to return north and fly the drop in tomorrow, forcing you to wait and risking more bad weather. And if I did drop food, the possibility of wind carrying the drop back onto the ice, or it landing in a dangerous area on the glacier is too much of a risk. Obviously, the biggest concern is another storm while you wait."

"How many days down the valley?" *Direction* asked.

"Four, maybe five, depending. And like I said, the farmer will give you a ride across the lake."

"So that's it; we hike out." *Direction* spoke with confidence as he calculated the risk.

"I suggest you all get moving, away from the ice."

That was the first thing I'd heard that sounded good: to get away from the ice and never return.

Change had been standing to my right. "What about helicopters?" he asked.

"The only helicopters in southern Chile are Army helicopters," *Positive* said. "And traditionally they haven't acted in civilian matters, even in emergencies."

Direction kept talking to the man in the plane. "Thanks for finding us, and tell that farmer we'll see him in a few days."

"Happy trails; tell your boys congratulations." The radio grew silent.

An eerie quiet overcame the group. No words needed to be spoken. We were the third expedition that had ever crossed the ice field, and yet, our new goal was still formidable. At that point, there was no need for breakfast, since we had no food. There was no need to break camp, because we had no tents. There was no need to do anything but stand and walk, stand and deliver.

◆◆◆

The man approached the farmer. He had just leaped from his motorized canoe, which was anchored to a tree two hundred yards along the lakeshore to the west. He was well dressed: jeans, dark blue long-sleeve shirt, working boots, a bright red baseball cap, and pilot glasses. He stood six feet, two inches tall and sported a well-groomed mustache. The farmer noticed and instantly liked the man's oversized, shiny silver belt buckle. The man reached out his hand. The farmer shook it politely.

"Hello," the man said.

"Hello," the farmer responded.

"I understand you have a farm here in this valley, and you run cattle up the valley toward Patagonia during the summer months."

"Yes."

The man pulled a wad of money from his pocket. "I need a favor." The farmer glanced at the money. "I have a group of men coming off the ice field in the next week, and I'll need you to give 'em a lift by canoe to the eastern side of the lake." The man, hand outreached, offered the farmer the wad of money.

"They have been on the ice field?" the farmer asked.

"Yes, for about six weeks now—should come through here in no more than five or six days."

"My friend, go back to the north from where you came. My family has lived here for six generations, working this land and raising cattle. I am sorry, but the storm that just came through here was the worst in the last one hundred and fifty years. Your friends are dead. Go back to the north and forget them."

"Oh no, I assure you they are alive."

"Friend, no person on this earth could have survived the winds and snow that just crossed that ice field—no man, no matter how strong." He paused, and looked east up the valley and toward the Patagonian Ice Field. "Up there, people die all the time in much lesser storms."

"I assure you, they lived," stated the man.

"How can you be so sure?"

"While flying a search-and-rescue mission over the region, I saw them!" The man's hand was still outreached, still offering the money.

"Oh my friend, I am sorry, but you saw dead bodies."

"They survived. I spoke with them by radio. They're very much alive. Please take the money; they'll need a ride in your boat."

"Oh, no problem for me. I'll give them a ride—your money is not needed."

"Thank you." The man turned and walked back to his boat.

◆◆◆

The temperature had steadily increased throughout the day as we dropped over four thousand feet down the valley and away from the ice field. The valley was dry and hot. Tall, multicolored sandstone cliffs rose majestically toward the sky, growing taller as the valley dropped in elevation. The terrain was steep, with no trails, or easy, obvious routes. There was a small stream that gained in size as we ventured down the valley. By late afternoon, it would become a river. As we maneuvered the valley, our main obstacles were bushes, unstable rocks, and many miniature cliffs.

This was our third day with no food. The last two days had been grueling, strenuous hikes. Again and again, I had watched my fellows struggle to find any remaining bits of energy, deep in their bodies. And every time, each one of us continued onward, sometimes slowly, sometimes painfully, but all nine of us kept moving forward.

It was nearing sundown and we were searching for a campsite for the night. I rounded a bend in the river to see *Persistence* and *Action* sprawled out on a huge sandbar. They looked like corpses.

I approached the two. "Is this home for the night?" I asked, while scratching my dry, but very hairy face.

Action looked at me with a blank face.

"Good a spot as any," *Persistence* said. Only his lips moved, while his eyes remained closed.

I fell backward onto my butt. I was far too tired to remove my pack and lie down. I stared blankly straight into the river, mesmerized by the effortless motion of the water.

How does the water move with so little effort? Amazing! I had been struggling with movement and obstacles all day.

Positive, *Worry*, and *Change* walked past me in a clump of movement. My gaze fixated on the water. *Slack* emerged from a bush to my right, with twigs and brush mixed into his hair. He stumbled toward me.

"I'm hungry," *Persistence* said.

Slack collapsed at my feet, landing on his knees. "I got an idea for food," he said.

Persistence rolled his head, looking toward us. Out of the same bush where *Slack* had just stumbled, *Direction* and *Everyday* came thrashing through the leaves and twigs. *Everyday's* ponytail was carrying a branch. The two fell to the ground twenty feet to our left.

Persistence rolled onto his side, facing *Slack* and me. "Food ideas are really good when we're starving," he said. "Please tell me you're serious."

"We've got over a hundred bags of garbage, little crumbs, old butter containers, old cheese scraps, rice, beans—all that stuff," *Slack* said.

"I looked the other day; it's rotting, and moldy, and smelly—and most of the bags look like shit or puke, or both," I said.

"That's your idea—to eat moldy trash?" *Persistence* said.

"We boil it," *Slack* said.

"Boiled garbage?"

They continued to chatter and I dug through my pack, pulling out my garbage. As I threw the bags near my feet, both *Slack* and *Action* began to dig through their garbage bags.

"You three can't be serious," *Persistence* said. "Didn't someone like four weeks ago puke in one of the bags when they were sick?"

"We'll boil it really good," *Slack* answered.

"Throw lots of spice into the stew, and it actually might work," I added.

"I just need something for energy; anything is better than nothing," *Slack* said.

Persistence struggled to his knees and started fishing in his pack. "Ah, what the hell; it's not like I have anything in my stomach to throw up."

◆◆◆

The sun was gone. Dusk had settled down thick. I looked into the clear night sky, enjoying, if only for a brief moment, the constellations in the southern hemisphere. We were spread across the sandbar in three separate groups. I was analyzing the Southern Cross.

Slack and *Persistence* sat Indian style next to a burning stove. To their right was a pile of smelly, rotting garbage bags. One by one, they had placed the small garbage bags into the warming water, removing every little speck of mold, and crumbs, and grime, and rot, and germs, and most important, nutrients.

"How long should we boil it?" *Persistence* asked.

"After I add these spices, probably another few minutes." *Slack* had just placed salt, pepper, basil, garlic powder, lemon pepper, oregano, chili powder, thyme, and green tea into a clean bag and was waiting to dump it into the garbage stew once it was boiling.

A few minutes passed, and silence crept across our camp. As the stove boiled the conglomeration of muck, I was transfixed on the stove's flame. It was easy to stare while starving.

"That should be long enough," *Slack* finally said.

"More spice," *Action* pleaded, as he covered his nose from the stinky steam.

"Not sure it matters," I said.

"I agree, let's eat," *Slack* said.

"This isn't going to resemble eating," *Persistence* said.

"Hand me your cup," *Slack* said to *Persistence.*

"I'm not going first?"

"I'll eat first." I handed my bowl to *Slack*.

He lifted the pot of grime and poured me a full bowl of garbage stew. I looked into the chunky, brown mixture. I swirled it around once; it resembled warm, bubbly sewage. As a full whiff penetrated my nostrils, I started to gag, but held back. One thing was certain: I had not eaten for three days, and if this did not kill me, it was bound to give me some nourishment.

"Here goes nothing," I said, lifting the bowl to my lips and slurping the chunky, brown stew into my mouth. I swallowed, definitely making sure not to chew any of it. "Eh, not that bad."

Oh man! That's the vilest crap I've ever tasted.

"You'll be fine," I said to *Persistence*. "Give it a taste."

Slack poured garbage stew into the other three bowls. I leaned back, looking forward to some entertainment before I slept on the sandbar.

February 28, 1996

The sun began to creep slowly over the eastern horizon. We had been hiking for two hours. The valley was flat. We had lost the majority of the elevation the previous day. Most of the time, we stayed near the river.

I was walking next to *Slack* and behind *Persistence.* "I just want to remind you both, I was the only one who didn't puke last night." I laughed.

"All I'm saying is you could've at least warned us," *Persistence* said, looking back at *Slack* for reassurance.

"Yeah maybe, but my way was much more fun," I said, giving *Slack's* backpack a playful nudge.

"For who?" *Persistence* asked.

"For me!" I said

"Hey, once I puked a few times, that stew stayed in my belly, and it actually did me good," *Slack* said.

"Not sure it did me good," I said. "But I did crap this morning for the first time in days, and it smelled like chili powder and garlic salt."

◆◆◆

All nine of us were sprawled motionless in an open field. The first shimmer of stars could be seen. We had covered thirty miles of the valley and with no trails to follow. Navigation was simple: head east, stay low in the valley, and hug the river as close as possible. If anything got in our path, like another river, a swamp, hillside, or landslide, we either went around, under, or through it. Most of the day we hiked in silence; energy was scarce. And we all knew we had at least two more days of hiking, possibly three, before we reached the valley's head. We had no need for a kitchen, because we had no more garbage to boil. Five minutes after we finished hiking, we simply passed out.

February 29, 1996

My eyes opened. I lay motionless as a fallen scarecrow, moist dew sprinkled over my clothing. A piece of grass swayed across my check, and I swatted at it as if it was a fly. I stood. A patch of grass the size of my body was compressed against the earth. I had slept in the open air, with no sleeping bag and no sleeping pad. The nine of us were spread out like a small herd of elk throughout the tall grass. If starvation and fatigue weren't so abundant, I would have found the scene peaceful.

Over a five-minute period, my peers crawled from the ground. When I stood, my feet began to pulse with sharp pain, like acid on the skin. The morning was draped in a thick veil of delusion. My mind was in a haze.

Everyday and *Direction* lifted their packs onto their backs. "Stay on the left, or north side, of the river today," *Direction* said. "Thirty-five miles downstream, another river joins this one; we'll sleep there tonight. Stay with at least with one other person—nobody hikes alone." And with that, *Everyday* and *Direction* walked toward the river shore and began their hiking day. *Slack* quickly followed.

It was nearly impossible to stay in a group of nine. All of us experienced different energy levels during the day. It was best to hike hard when energy was available, and when starvation was ruling the pace, inches at time would have to suffice.

I looked down at my pack and briefly lost track of time, until *Worry* tapped me on the shoulder. He and I were the only two left in the field.

"Let's go," *Worry* said.

◆◆◆

For most of the day, I had been hiking with *Direction*, *Slack*, *Positive*, and *Everyday*. We had found a trail, and for the last half mile, had been following its course. About an hour prior, our group got a glimpse of *Action*, *Worry*, *Persistence*, and *Change* on an open patch of ground about a quarter mile in front of us. The day had been long. We guessed we had already covered thirty of the thirty-five miles. I had not spoken a word for hours.

The five of us rounded a turn in the trial. One hundred yards in the distance was an old and eerie-looking barn. We continued to hike toward it. As we came around the back corner of the barn, there was a rustic, half-collapsed log cabin in an open field. We walked next to the fence line until we came to an opening and crossed over into what was once the backyard of the log cabin.

"This's the old winter shelter of the cattle rancher who lives at the valley's head," *Direction* said. "They'd stay here when they ran cattle up the valley during the winter months."

"Think they left any pizza or beer in the refrigerator?" *Everyday* asked.

"I wish, but that right there's an apple tree," *Positive* said, pointing to a nearby tree.

"There's not an apple on it," *Everyday* said.

"Just our luck," *Slack* said, while scratching his stomach

through a hole in his ragged shirt.

"Let's take five minutes to rest," *Direction* said.

"I can't," *Slack* said. "If I stop, my legs won't move anymore."

"I'll keep moving with *Slack*; you guys stop if you want to," *Positive* said.

Slack and *Positive* disappeared into a cluster of trees on the far side of the property. I walked to the apple tree.

"Not a single damn apple," I said.

I grabbed one of the low-hanging apple tree branches. The other two sat near the back side of the log cabin. I needed to eat something, anything, and so, one by one, I began to eat leaves, like a giraffe, straight from the branch of the apple tree.

"How is that?" *Everyday* asked.

"Good, but there's a reason they sell apples at the store and not the leaves," I said, with my mouth full of leaves. "But I don't care; I'm eating."

Everyday stood and walked across the small patch of grass to join me at the apple tree. He grabbed a branch and started to eat.

"Not bad," *Everyday* said, as he grazed on the tree leaves. "*Direction*, you should give this a shot."

"I'm better off with nothing in my stomach but water," *Direction* said, as he lifted his water bottle to his mouth and drank.

He wouldn't say that if I had a fat, juicy steak. But then again, I wouldn't be chewing leaves from a tree like a panda.

Direction stood back up. "Let's get going. Watching you two gnaw at that tree is depressing."

Tree firmly in hand, working my way down the branch

like a piece of corn, I looked at *Direction* out of the corners of my eyes. For the first time in my life, I was an animal, a true beast, surviving solely on instincts. I would kill to eat.

March 1, 1996

I awoke to the sound of two rivers. It was the start of day seven with no real food. I was told it was March the second. But I had not seen my journal for weeks. I rolled to my side. We had slept in a tight clump that night. I was one of the last ones to awaken from my coma like sleep. The rest of the guys were sitting on the ground, or leaning against their packs. They all seemed methodical in their lack of motion.

"This should be it. Last day," *Direction* said, looking down river.

We had maps of the valley, but the lower valley had been permanently altered ten years prior when a massive landslide released all the water of a high alpine lake. And the ensuing flood had changed the valley's terrain dramatically. Reading the map was close to impossible.

"The valley head should be on the other side of that hill," *Direction* said, referring to a hill that looked to be seven miles away and two hundred feet off the valley floor.

Worry, *Change*, *Everyday*, and *Positive* stood, lifted their packs, and began a slow and uneasy walk away from the rest of us. It looked like they were walking on the nubs of their legs, as if they had just had both feet amputated. The pain on their faces told me amputation would have been a good option. Each time one of their feet would touch the ground, their faces would pucker with pain. Twice, *Worry* sat back down onto the ground. The nerves in our feet were severely damaged.

"They look like hell," I said.

"Couldn't be any worse than the last month," *Persistence* said.

"Let's go," *Slack* said. "I want to get this over with."

We stood. Like a nuclear explosion, the pain rippled and swelled in a massive tidal wave from my feet, through my lower body, and exploded from the top of my skull. For a moment, I hoped to die. The pain in my feet was tremendous.

I looked at *Worry*. He appeared to be on the verge of vomiting.

Direction lifted his backpack, throwing it over his shoulder. "I guess the pain means were not dead yet," *Direction* said without emotion.

"Let's go," *Slack* said again. "I want to get this over with."

I started to walk. I felt like I was walking on fire. Twenty minutes into the hike, my feet slowly began to lose their feeling. The burning sensation had vanished; what remained felt like the balls of my feet were steel, and the ground where I walked was steel, and with every step, they violently clanged and collided together. I could feel my body starting to digest itself, like a snake eating its tail, working its way around and up to its own head.

◆◆◆

It was early afternoon and we had been on the move for six hours. The day had been a carnival of pain, so many variations. We came to a slight hill, no more than two hundred feet in elevation. In mountaineering terms, a drop of water in a bucket, a grain of sand on a beach, a piece of straw in a haystack. Most any day, two hundred feet would be nothing, like climbing a household ladder. But this was not any day. I had not eaten food for seven days, and during those seven days, I had hiked, on average, over twelve hours a day. Prior to that, I had eaten limited food for ten days while rotting and freezing in the ice. And even before the storm, I had punished my body with the highest level of physical exercise my muscles had ever experienced. There's a race in Hawaii called the Iron Man. The racers swim in the open ocean for two point five miles, and then ride a bike for one hundred and twelve miles, all followed by a full marathon of twenty-six point two miles. I desperately wished for something as easy as doing the Iron Man with a fresh body in comparison to climbing these last two hundred feet.

Mountaineering is exciting and romantic? Yeah, right! Screw those extreme commercials I see on television, lying to the general public. Mountaineering is hell.

Slack approached from behind and stopped. He looked at me, or tried to look at me, his eyes crossed. He appeared to be on the verge of collapsing. After a few moments, he regained focus.

"If I live, I'm moving to Nebraska; it's flat in that state," *Slack* said. "No hills."

Before I could respond, *Persistence* walked up to our left. He stopped, wiped the sweat from his forehead, and looked up the hill. "Well—" He paused midthought and looked to his right at both *Slack* and me, then returned his focus back to the hill. "Come this far in life; might as well climb one more hill." *Persistence* walked forward.

Leave it to Persistence to get me over the final hill.

No better time than now. I started to follow, walking behind the back left hip of *Persistence*. My legs crept forward. I watched an ant on the ground pass me, but I was moving forward. Pain blasted me, and I was lost. My mental blender had been turned to high, and millions of thoughts and memories blended into mush.

Out of the cauldron, one thought rose to the surface: Thirty days prior, my leader named *Direction* had told me of *Cowboy Now,* his Mother *Nature*, and the calf called *Life*. *Cowboy Now* discovered that the best way to rope *Life* was to focus on what part of *Life* he wanted to rope, forget about everything else, disregard the doubters, ignore the possibility of failure, and for that exact moment in time, let the lasso do its job.

The hill crested. We were at the valley's head. That was the last hill. I had roped *Life*.

◆◆◆

I walked to the lakeshore. Once there, I looked from side to side. The afternoon sun was bright and warm. *Direction* was to my left; we were first out of the tree's canopy. I looked over to him, no emotion from either of us. Part of me was shocked that we had not erupted with a scream, or dance, or some form of celebration. The other part of me understood. We were done. I dropped my backpack.

I laid my limp body on my pack, and one by one, I watched my friends emerge from the trees. Nothing, not one single sign of success, of a job well done, or even a slight smile. The nine of us were physically, mentally, and emotionally exhausted. Thoroughly famished with nothing left to give.

I turned back toward the lake. A Chilean farmer approached in a large motorized canoe. He waved at us, grinning from ear to ear. His toothless smile was huge. He aimed the canoe toward the shore and ran it aground. From the hull of the boat, out jumped a medium-sized dog. The dog twisted and turned in dog happiness while waiting for his owner.

Hmm! What a cute dog? Let's eat it!

Survival overrides anything and everything. My stomach controlled my brain. I was starving. I looked at *Direction.* He stood and moved toward the farmer.

Hey, bring me back some BBQ dog, please!

Direction and the farmer shook hands, exchanged pleasantries. The farmer pointed up the valley toward the ice field, and then back at the lake. *Direction* patiently stood, arms crossed, silent, just listening to the farmer.

How does he do that? I don't have the energy to listen!

After another few minutes, *Direction* spun backward, returning to his pack. He stood by my feet for a few moments in thought. I looked up at him, while the sun seemed to put a halo around his head. I squinted, holding my hand out to block the sun.

Direction spoke as he gazed up the valley: "Farmer said we should be dead."

No shit! My body was dead limp, draped over the backside of my backpack.

He continued. "Said that's the worst weather ever to come through these parts." *Direction* grabbed his pack and lifted it to his back. "Let's go."

Worst weather ever to come through these parts? Hmm. And somewhere, in some book, I remember reading that Patagonia's got the worst weather system in the world. Worst weather, biggest storm, in the worst weather in the world. I need to find another hobby!

◆◆◆

I was the last person in the large canoe. The rest of the guys were standing on the wooden dock. I struggled with my pack. It settled to the bottom of the canoe.

Not sure I feel like moving!

"You need help?" *Everyday* asked, looking at me from the dock.

"No, I got it," I answered. "That boat ride put me to sleep; now my body's really struggling."

"Hand it to me," he said.

I stood, wobbled slightly, unsure if it was the boat or my equilibrium, and after balancing myself, grabbed the straps of my pack. For a moment, I struggled to lift it, but eventually I raised it to my right knee. At that point, *Everyday* grabbed the top and pulled it to the dock. I crawled out of the boat. The farmer waved goodbye. I tried to smile. I tried to care.

Direction was looking over the shore. We were at a little town, maybe five or ten houses. "Let's go to that tree. We can organize and wait there." *Direction* pointed to a large oak tree, with soft, green grass under it. He walked to a nearby house.

The group slowly shuffled the fifty yards to the oak tree. I dropped to the ground, as we created circle.

God the grass feels good.

Direction returned with a bag full of bread and cheese. "Here, pass this around. Should tide us over until the truck gets here tomorrow morning."

We ate cheese and bread. Our stomachs had shrunk so much that after one bread roll and one hunk of cheese, I was full. My body absorbed the nutrients instantly. I could feel the energy. After one hour of rest and silence, the bread and cheese were passed once more around the circle.

Positive sat up. He took a long swig of water. "We could have lasted another week, maybe two," he said. "We all need to understand that. As beaten, and tired, and miserable as we feel, we could've survived longer."

Not a word was said. I stared blankly at a tree behind him.

Positive continued. “I think we should begin to debrief, while the feeling is fresh. Start to process our experience, understand what just happened to us.”

I gazed over his head, miles away, far off into the distance, to where an eagle soared high into the deep blue sky. People began to talk and I listened, never quite sure whose voice I heard, but in reality, it didn’t matter. The nine of us were the same. We were all human and we were all survivors. I was a combination of my peers, a combination of all things good, and all things not so good. I was human. I listened, and in truth, it made all the difference in the world.

Here I am today, alive and well. I'm the same man I was before Patagonia, only with a different view of life. I have been asked many, many times how I survived. Simple: Survival was my only choice, my only option. That, or dying, and when death is near, it never looks appealing or seems like a good direction. Sadly, two hundred miles to the south of the northern ice field, in a separate region of Patagonia, six men died during that same massive blizzard. They were exposed to the elements, stranded on a six thousand–foot rock face called Torres del Paine. The blizzard killed them. They had no shelter from the storm. I had a cave. I hated my cave. I lived because of my cave.

I have also been asked countless times what I learned from the experience of surviving in a snow cave. Bottom line, I learned it's sometimes easier to survive in a snow cave when that's your only choice than to survive and prosper in life when there's the freedom of choice.

On that last day of the journey, after we'd crossed the lake and as we sat under that massive oak tree, we all talked. At that point, we all knew we'd survived. The journey was over and life was about to return. These are the ideas we discussed under that oak tree on the eastern side of Patagonia. These are my new mantras for my life after living, battling, and surviving in a snow cave on the Northern Patagonian Ice Field:

- Life can always be roped, whether you're young, old, or a Cowboy named Now.

- When in a storm on the Northern Patagonian Ice Field, don't pretend to be on a beach in the South of France. Live where you sleep. Deal with the issue at hand.
- Don't judge value based on some other person's value system. You may end up with no toes and a Big Mac.
- If you have friends who are doves, let them hatch their own eggs. Life is better learned through experience.
- When in doubt, follow *Direction.*
- Everyone has a purpose. Even if it's not in line with your purpose, it's their purpose and their path. *Persistence*, *Slack*, *Change*, *Action*, *Direction*, *Worry*, *Positive*, *Everyday*, and *Today* all have a purpose. And together they create life.
- At first, *Change* is a dick. In the end, *Change* can be your best friend.
- All the aspects of today are possible in every single moment. If *Today* is well lived, memories will be great and tomorrow will be bright.
- Sometimes when you're in hell, God is near. Sometimes when you're in heaven, God's on a trip to hell. So pay attention to who's to the left and right of you.
- We are all human. We are all born into this world. And we will all die of this world.
- Needs and wants are relative based on your expectations.
- In life, you'd better be someone who prays or else one lucky bastard. Believe in both!
- When the storm's at its greatest, stay sheltered, warm, and rested. When the storm breaks, crawl up and out, and then don't stop moving forward until you reach your goal.
- Life is precious! Life is gold!
- Never underestimate the power of patience and persistence.
- One life—make your move.

Sir Ernest Hemingway once stated that if all stories continue far enough, they end in death, and to be a true storyteller, one must write this honestly.

I agree: Someday I will die. Someday. Patagonia did not kill (all of) me, and in fact, awakened (most of) me. Inevitably, I will die someday in the future. But now, I am alive, and until I die, I will crawl up and out everyday of my life between this moment and my last.

ACKNOWLEDGMENTS

I would like to clarify the Acknowledgments for all those who don't understand the entire process of creating, and then publishing, a book (prior to writing *Cowboy Now*, I was one of them). The following people helped bring this book to life; without them, this story would never have had a chance to find print. Geoff, through all of *Cowboy Now*'s early drafts, provided the perfect sounding board. Nancy edited my work skillfully, without editing out my story. Valerie supplied me with the means to continue my pursuit of publication. Stacy, my fiancée, helped guide my desire. All the friends of Bill continue to keep me focused. And every single person who's had a dream, chased that dream, and succeeded; I was watching.